RESEARCH GUIDE FOR UNDERGRADUATES IN
political science

Carl Kalvelage
Morley Segal
Peter J. Anderson

GENERAL LEARNING PRESS

Library of Congress Card Number: 78-185110

Acknowledgements

Certain material included in this book is copyrighted by the authors and publishers of the following citations. The use of these editions is gratefully acknowledged.

Congressional Quarterly Weekly Report. Washington, D.C.: Congressional Quarterly, Inc., 28 November 1969.

Editor & Publisher Magazine. New York: Editor & Publisher, 5 November 1960; 31 October 1964; 2 November 1968.

Segal, Morley and Kalvelage, Carl. *Study Guide for Stephen V. Monsma's American Politics: A Systems Approach.* New York: Holt, Rinehart & Winston, Inc., 1970.

Somit, Albert and Tanenhaus, Joseph. *American Political Science.* New York: Atherton Press, Inc., 1964.

Contents

PART III

Preface

According to psychologists, most of us will forget over 90 percent of the facts we learn in college within five years of graduation. That is, of course, if we choose to never review the material by thinking or reading about it. But even if we were gifted with total recall, the facts would have changed so much in five years that they'd be barely recognizable. For example, the population of the United States as of 1971 is 205 million; the figure used for 1966 is more than 10 million off the target.

This research guide is designed to keep the undergraduate on target. It's a device to help the political science undergraduate while in college and after graduation; it directs the student to source material that will give or restore knowledge in the field; it tells how to organize and document a research paper; suggests how to use the library as a source of ideas for picking a topic; it contains advice and encouragement for those who have difficulty in formulating a hypothesis and drawing up an outline. Finally, the text contains a number of unique items to which the average undergraduate in political science will not generally be exposed (e.g., the scope and biases of the top political columnists, a ranking of political scientists, a ranking of political science departments, etc.).

The source list provided herein is designed to give depth and sustenance to undergraduate courses in political science. It doesn't pretend to be exhaustive or even comprehensive at the graduate level; rather, it is limited to the main source materials, to those references with which every good undergraduate student in this field should be familiar.

We believe that the student will find this research guide adequate for even the most demanding undergraduate paper in the area of political science. We regret that there was no such guide in our own undergraduate days.

Carl Kalvelage
Morley Segal
Peter J. Anderson

PART I

How To Research And Write A Topic in Political Science

The research paper is one of the basic tools of scholarship. It is the written result of careful investigation of a chosen topic and is intended to display simultaneously the student's grasp of the topic and his ability to express himself in a scholarly fashion.

The completion of a research paper to the instructor's satisfaction indicates a tour de force by the student that transcends the rote of simple recall and is a badge assuring some expertise in the chosen subject. The instructor may also be assured that his student has learned where and how to search out information; how to use the library; how to take accurate notes; how to support ideas with footnotes; how to list a bibliography so that others may turn to cited sources; and most important, how to organize his thoughts on a given topic.

In political science, as in every discipline, the research paper is a scholar's credentials; credentials that must be earned. And to this end the following suggestions are offered as aids to choosing, researching, and writing a topic in political science.

UNDERSTANDING THE TOPIC

If the instructor should assign a topic, the student's first step clearly must be to familiarize himself with that topic. This endeavor should lead him to the relevant pages of the class text, to some other introductory text, or to a general or subject encyclopedia, handbook, glossary, etc. At this point, the *International Encyclopedia of the Social Sciences* is helpful.

If, on the other hand, the choice of topic is left to the student (the rule in college rather than the exception), he must be prepared for an intellectual struggle. For selecting an initial topic can be a time-consuming and frustrating task. An entire section (pp. 10-19) therefore, has been devoted to helping the individual choose an enjoyable and manageable topic.

OUTLINING THE PROJECT

Working from the supposition that a topic has already been selected, the next step is to make a statement of purpose, revealing as precisely as possible the intention of the writer. Where does he plan to direct his topic; how does he plan to treat it generally, with what approach and to what end? Each word of this statement should be scrutinized for exact meaning.

Then, on the basis of a preliminary survey of the topic, a rough outline is prepared, an outline that is divided into as many chapters and subchapters as possible. Here, for the first time, the various angles of the topic to be investigated are listed. And it is this incipient outline that will be the student's constant guide for research — constant, but never unalterable. An outline is a skeleton, rather, of the final report, to which may be added or from which may be deleted material for the final draft. There are several strong reasons for constructing this outline (none of which is the didactic whim of the instructor), but the strongest is that it gives direction to all subsequent research.

PREPARING A BIBLIOGRAPHY

The best point of departure in preparing a bibliography is the bibliography in the class text, using those titles that appear to deal directly with the assigned or selected topic. Next, the student simply checks the library to see if those books or journals or pamphlets are in stock; this is most easily done by examining the card catalogue files kept by all libraries — alphabetized by authors, titles and subjects, with all books listed in each.

The periodicals can be covered through the indexes and abstracts that are kept scrupulously up-to-date by librarians. The index lists information such as where and when the article was published, while the abstract gives this information plus a brief resume of the article's contents. References such as these are arranged by author, title, subject, or even a combination of all these. Examples of indexes are *Reader's Guide to Periodical Literature* (p. 74); *Public Affairs Information Service Index* (p. 74); *Humanities and Social Science Index* p. 76); *The New York Times Index* (p. 72).

These sources, since they refer to journals and magazine articles rather than published book-length treatments, are the sources of the freshest material.

Should the topic selected be what is known in journalism circles as a breaking story — that is to say, a topic that is ongoing and developing from day to day — then the student may find materials published by the Federal government or by the United Nations of invaluable help. Whatever the case, whatever the nature of the topic, there is a vast supply of books, magazines, pamphlets, tracts, and other relevant documents ready to add depth and direction to scholarly research.

The best and easiest way to prepare a bibliography is to use 4x6 or 5x8 index cards, lined or unlined, on which to note the pertinent data. Across the top of these cards is written the name of the author, title of the book, the edition, place of publication, publisher, date of publication and volume number.

If the material is contained in a journal, the necessary data include the author, title of the article, name of the journal, volume number, date of publication, place of publication, and the page numbers covering the article. In either case, the library classification number should be added. A separate card, of course, should be used for each entry.

CHECKING THE BIBLIOGRAPHY

Once the bibliography is compiled, it becomes urgent to determine if the volumes and journals listed are, indeed, available in the library. And if they are, then the student must scan them to be certain that they contain material relevant to the topic.

Using the library classification numbers, the student can go directly to the shelf where a check of the chapter contents or the index of a volume will determine if it can be of use. If this proves positive, then a notation on the index card should explain in what way it can be used.

TAKING NOTES

Now the material gathered by the student must be read and from it all pertinent information extracted. The resultant research notes should be transcribed clearly and concisely on index cards, each card marked with the title of the book or journal.

When an author is paraphrased, care should be taken to assure that his intent is not distorted; when quoting, the quote must be exact. Notes generally should be as brief as is practical, but should they run to length, the student will serve himself well to number each card used in sequence.

Finally, when the note is completed, a record should be made of the page or pages where the material was found.

PUTTING IT ALL TOGETHER

The original material has now been read and gleaned of all material that will give some form to the preliminary skeletal outline. It is all there on the index cards, waiting to be shaped by the student. He should read the notes carefully, gaining in this manner a comprehensive overview of his material; he should become aware of supporting and contradicting material, and then — using the rough draft as a guide — he should begin mentally building the essay step by step from the information amassed.

It is at this point that the student may decide that his material indicates that a new or different tack should be taken, that it is advisable to alter the original outline, perhaps drastically, or that he was on target right from the start. Whatever the decision, a final outline is cast, the one on which the facts of the research must ultimately hang. And when the dust has cleared, that new outline should contain the main theme, a list of points to be emphasized, and the placement of those points in the finished paper. It is ready to be written.

WRITING THE PAPER

The preceding six steps have lead to the actual writing of the first draft of the essay, and there are easily a hundred ways of attacking this task. The simplest is for the student to know what he wants to say about his topic and then to say it simply and directly. Clarity is important; when the paper is finished, there ought to be no mistaking its intent.

Setting down in order all the material gathered is not enough. The writing must reflect the writer; that is to say, it should be imbued with his thoughts on the topic, his questions of the material used, his intellectual strength in bringing opposite opinions face to face.

To wind up the demands of form, the student must remember that when quotations, opinions or statistics are woven into the fabric of the essay, they must be acknowledged through a footnote. Also, the completed paper must contain a title page at the beginning, and a bibliography at the end.

Form of the Paper

To grasp a handy maxim, neatness counts. It would be almost cavalier to spend all the time and energy that a good paper demands, and then produce a sloppy, nonuniform, slipshod copy for the instructor.

Usually an instructor requires that the paper have a suitable cover, and that its parts be arranged in a logically flowing sequence; a sequence such as the following is generally found acceptable:

I. The title page, uniformly spaced, must bear the following information.
   Title of the paper in capital letters
   Student's name
   Course designation
   School name
   Date
II. Dedication (optional).
III. The preface (also optional) usually acknowledges any debts the writer incurred in researching his topic.
IV. The table of contents should be on a separate page and should offer the name of each chapter or division, any appendixes used, and the bibliography. Each of these sections is to be identified by the page number of the paper where they are to be found. Frequently a paper is not divided into chapters and contains no index, and so it follows that a table of contents is unnecessary.

V. Illustrations, if used, should be listed on a separate page and otherwise treated as the table of contents is treated.

VI. The manuscript, itself, should be neatly typed on one side of white standard 8x11 paper. Corrected typographical errors usually are acceptable but too many make the product unworthy of the time and work invested. The body of type should be arranged neatly on each page, with plenty of room at the top and bottom and at each margin.

The text should be double-spaced, but single-spaced verse, extended prose quotations, and footnotes are conventional. Should a quote run less than two typewritten lines, quotation marks are used.

Finally, the page numbers, including those of the appendix and bibliography, are marked in arabic numerals in the upper right corner.

VII. Preparing the footnotes and bibliography usually causes the undergraduate much grief. A separate section, therefore, has been devoted to this area (pp. 20).

Selecting A Topic

Selecting an initial topic can be a time-consuming and frustrating task. The problem is one of developing a focus which is both interesting and workable. Hours and hours may be spent trying to formulate an approach or researching what turns out to be an unworkable topic. A topic that may be interesting ("How to Prevent World War III") is not always manageable; that which may be manageable ("Bolivia and American Tin Quotas") might not stir the imagination.

It is important to select a topic that is interesting, not only as it is originally conceived, but one which continues to hold interest through the hard task of research. Choosing a topic and scanning the sources are not separate tasks; they are entwined — doing one helps in doing the other. In this section three important steps are presented leading to developing an interesting and workable topic.

A PRACTICAL FORMULA FOR CHOOSING A TOPIC

The first step in developing any formula is to define its elements; thus, one must first decide upon an initial area. To simplify this process possible research areas have been divided into two basic groups: the *abstract* and the *concrete*. These two general areas are further divided into subgroups.

To those who are completely lost, with no hint of even a possible topic, seven of the most fertile sources in a library are offered.

Facts on file: World News Digest
Congressional Quarterly
Foreign Affairs Bibliography
Public Affairs Information Service Index
Encyclopedia Yearbooks
Dissertations
National Party Platforms 1840-1960

The Concrete — Browsing For Ideas

There is a natural appeal to a concrete topic; that is to say, a topic concerned with a person, an entity or organization, an event or a law. If one has a predisposition to investigate something, it is likely to be one of the above concrete items. If the idea of such a topic is appealing, but it is difficult to choose which person or country would be most interesting, an hour or so of creative browsing may be rewarding. Simply thumbing through several of the resources listed on the following pages may bring several topics to mind. For convenience, these sources have been divided into four groups.

1. Persons
2. Entities (which includes the whole range of human organization from nations to neighborhood groups)
3. Events
4. Laws, programs, and policies

The most useful and general of these sources are listed in a separate section followed by the more specialized sources. In most cases the title will give a general description of the work. For a more detailed description as well as the bibliographic citation, refer to the page listed after each title.

A Person

The best general sources
Biography Index (note topical index in each volume) (p. 51)
Encyclopedia Yearbooks
Congressional Quarterly (p. 54)
Dictionary of American Biography (p. 59)
Current Biography (p. 57)

The more specialized sources
- *Congressional Directory* (p. 52)
- *Encyclopedia of the Social Sciences* (p. 63)
- *International Encyclopedia of the Social Sciences* (p. 63)
- *Essay and General Literature Index* (p. 64)
- *International Who's Who* (p. 70)
- Political Scientists: A Ranking (p. 87)
- *Taylor's Encyclopedia of Government Officials (Federal and State)* (p. 77)
- *Vital Speeches of the Day* (p. 80)
- *Who's Who in American Politics* (p. 81)
- The Top Twenty Political Columnists (p. 89)
- *Facts about the Presidents* (p. 64)
- *Dictionary of American Biography* (p. 59)

An Entity or Organization

The best general sources
- *United States Government Organization Manual* (p. 79)
- *Worldmark Encyclopedia of Nations* (p. 82)
- *Encyclopedia of Associations*
- *Yearbook of International Organizations* (p. 82)
- *National and International Interest Groups* (p. 94)

The more specialized sources
- *Book of the States* (p. 51)
- *Everyman's United Nations* (p. 64)
- Information Services in the United States of Members of the United Nations (p. 96)
- *Political Handbook and Atlas of the World* (p. 73)
- *Yearbook of the United Nations* (p. 83)
- Encyclopedia Yearbooks
- *Foreign Affairs Bibliography* (p. 65)
- *United States in World Affairs* (p. 80)
- *Comparative International Almanac* (p. 52)
- *Select Bibliography: Asia, Africa, Eastern Europe, Latin America* (p. 75)
- *American Agencies Interested in International Affairs* (p. 50)
- *Municipal Yearbook* (p. 71)

Events

Best general sources
- *Congressional Quarterly* (p. 54)
- *Congress and the Nation* (p. 54)
- Encyclopedia Yearbooks

An Encyclopedia of World History (p. 63)
Facts on File: World News Digest (p. 64)
The most specialized sources
America Votes (p. 50)
New York Times Index (p. 72)
World Almanac and Book of Facts (p. 82)
Foreign Affairs Bibliography (p. 65)
The Annual Register of World Events (p. 51)
Guide to the Diplomatic History of the United States (p. 67)

Laws, Policies, and Programs

The best general sources
Congressional Quarterly (p. 54)
Congress and the Nation (p. 54)
Subject Guide to Major Government Publications (p. 77)
National Party Platforms 1840-1960 (p. 72)
Yearbook of the United Nations (p. 83)
The more specialized sources
Everyman's United Nations (p. 64)
The Consititution of the United States of America: Analysis and Interpretation (p. 56)
Gallup Opinion Index (p. 73)
Municipal Yearbook (p. 71)
Public Affairs Information Service Index (p. 74)
Statistical Abstract of the United States (p. 77)
Treaties in Force (p. 78)
United States Government Organization Manual (p. 79)
United States Reports (p. 80)
Vital Speeches of the Day (p. 80)
Weekly Compilation of Presidential Documents (p. 81)
Universal Reference System (p. 80)

The Abstract — Browsing for Ideas

Classifying ideas and abstractions has been the pursuit of philosophers for centuries. Since the purpose of this book is to use ideas in a practical fashion to help focus and organize the proposed paper, a very simple three-fold classification will be adopted for abstract topics.

1. *Values*: ideas and concepts implying desirability
2. *Problems*: ideas and concepts implying undesirability
3. *Process*: ideas and concepts that imply neither desirability or undesirability

To be more explicit, "value" refers to any concept or idea that describes an interest, pleasure, moral obligation, desire, want, need, etc. It may refer to a measurable activity, like equal opportunity in employment, or to an intangible, such as "support for the regime."

Problem," the second organizational classification, may also refer to a measurable activity or a feeling, but it is generally regarded as an undesirable, such as a feeling of political alienation, or apathy.

"Process" has no connotation of desirability or undesirability but simply refers to any observable or definable pattern in activities of people and groups. "Political process" refers to the pattern that emerges from the behavior of people and groups as they strive for and use political power.

Many ideas or concepts can be placed in two or even all three of these categories — depending upon the intent of the holder. The radical ideas of Mark Rudd, for instance, can be treated as a neutral process, a grave problem, or a boon to the republic. How one regards these ideas depends upon his own attitudes. The categories of value, problem, and process simply help in identifying one's own feelings toward these ideas in order to use them in organizing a paper.

All three of the abstract concept classifications have one thing in common: as ideas, they cannot be seen, heard, or felt. Often they are not even recognized by those involved but are an abstraction imposed upon them by an outside observer (for example, the process of a group of grade school children saluting the flag). Neither these children nor their teacher may realize that they are involved in the "process of political socialization" but they would be observed as such by many political scientists.

Whatever one's preference for political description, these three categories of abstract ideas will be invaluable for organizing thoughts and ideas into a paper. Since most source books deal with ideas and concepts applicable to all three categories, they have been listed together. If a research source is especially relevant to one category, this has been indicated in parentheses.

Abstractions: Values, Problems, and Process

The best general source
   The *Syntopicon Volumes*
      Universal Reference System (p. 80)
      Masterpieces of World Philosophy in Summary Form (Values)
         (p. 71)

Public Affairs Information Service Index (especially for
    problems) (p. 74)
ABS Guide to Recent Publications in the Social and Behavioral
    Sciences (process) (p. 49)
International Encyclopedia of Social Sciences (p. 63)
Social Sciences and Humanities Index (p. 76)
Vital Speeches of the Day (p. 80)
Doctoral Dissertations in Political Science in Universities
    in the United States (p. 61)
The more specialized sources
Congressional Digest (p. 52)
The Constitution of the United States of America: Analysis
    and Interpretation (p. 56)
Essay and General Literature Index (p. 64)
Weekly Compilation of Presidential Documents (p. 81)
Index to Legal Periodicals (p. 69)
Foreign Affairs Bibliography (p. 65)
National Party Platforms 1840-1960 (problems) (p. 72)
Readers' Guide to Periodical Literature (p. 74)
Congressional Quarterly (p. 54)
Congress and the Nation (p. 54)
Subject Guide to Major Government Publications (p. 77)
Guide to Reference Material in Political Science (p. 66)

As one begins to explore the material it is usually discovered
that far more has been written on the chosen topic than expected.
The traditional advice is to "narrow" the topic, but this is only a
partial answer, for "narrowing" in the traditional way can squeeze
the life out of an interesting topic. The next section demonstrates
how to narrow a topic and still keep it interesting.

DEVELOPING THE TOPIC

What is usually called "narrowing down" refers to the process of
reducing a topic in terms of either time or space. Instead of writing
about Robert Kennedy's entire life, the topic may be reduced to the
months he spent working for Senator Joseph McCarthy. Instead of
writing about Mexican politics, a paper on politics in Sonora
province might be developed. The project now appears to become
manageable, but it may not be, actually, because one still may find
that there is far more written about politics in Sonora province or
about this period in Robert Kennedy's life than can be dealt with in

a term paper. When a topic is finally narrowed down, it often is so narrow that it becomes a task even to state the title. On the other hand, if it is decided not to narrow the topic down, often coverage is so superficial that originality is sacrificed.

Another choice is available in reducing a topic: that is, to develop a sharper focus in terms of interesting and worthwhile questions that might be answered about the chosen topic, questions that help to define what is relevant and what is not for research.

The problem is now to identify these questions. One method is to combine the categories of the abstract and concrete; for example, that topic of Robert Kennedy (concrete) and the idea of "Black Power" (an abstract value). There are a great many possible combinations of these categories. To help in identifying some of the possibilities for a selected topic, three charts have been constructed:

1. Combining the concrete and the abstract
2. Combining one abstraction with another
3. Combining two concrete objects

Tables 1, 2 and 3 develop these possibilities further.

Table 1 Combining the concrete and the abstract

	Process	Problem	Value
Person	Richard Nixon and the introduction of P.P.B.S. budgeting	Gen. Lewis Hershey and the alienation of American youth	Will Rogers and the development of American political satire
Event	The election of 1928 and the growth of the New Deal coalition	The Treaty of Versailles and the rise of Adolph Hitler	The War of 1812 and the tradition of political dissent
Entity	The Sierra Club and the mobilization of public opinion on conservation	The Irish Republican Army (IRA) and violence in Northern Ireland	The Anti-Federalists and the development of the idea of citizen participation in administration
Law or Policy	Aid to Latin America and the congressional appropriations process	The first amendment and the problem of obscenity in the mail	FHA and the development of the idea of a "stake in society"

Table 2 Combining two abstractions as a focus

	Process	*Problem*	*Value*
Process	The conflict between internal congressional and constituent pressures upon Congresswoman Shirley Chisholm	The election of federal judges and the problems of conflict of interest	The development of political attitudes in the comic strip "Peanuts"
Problem	Presidential press relations: the problem of Lyndon Johnson	Organized crime, wiretapping and the right of privacy	Rational choice in presidential elections and the threat of television image-making
Value	The impact of capital punishment on prison discipline	Adam Clayton Powell, and the right of Congress to expel its members	Speed vs. thoroughness: drug testing problems of F.D.A.

Table 3 Combining two concrete objects of study on the basis of an abstraction

	Person	Event	Entity	Law or Policy
Person	Eugene McCarthy and Hubert Humphrey as freshman senators: a comparison	Harold Stassen and the Republican Convention of 1948	George Wallace and his impact on organized labor	U Thant and the development of U.N. police action
Event	Mayor Richard Daley and the election of John F. Kennedy in 1960	A comparison of two campaigns: Henry Wallace 1948, George Wallace 1968	The A.M.A. and defeat of Medicare in 1961	The Farmers' Holiday and the growth of agricultural price supports
Entity	Robert McNamara and the reorganization of the Department of Defense	The American Legion and the Viet Nam War	Kenya and Tanzania: a comparison of electoral process	The Office of Passports and Communist Cuba
Law or Policy	Secretary of Interior Udall and the Development of the new conservation	The Open Housing Law and the election of Ronald Reagan as Governor of California	The Neighborhood Legal Service and the city government of Chicago	Two approaches to rural poverty: Department of Agriculture and the Office of Economic Opportunity

Footnotes and Bibliography

FOOTNOTES

Few aspects of writing cause as much confusion, bewilderment, and frustration as the proper use of footnotes. Footnotes are an essential part of scholarly writing, but until the fundamentals of their use are mastered, the footnote requirement can be a constant source of frustration. As a writing device footnotes are useful because they allow important information to be communicated without overburdening the text. More specifically, footnotes allow a writer to reflect both credit and blame where they are due by showing the source of facts and ideas, thereby permitting the reader to utilize cited sources. In addition, footnotes act as a helpful context for presented information, indicating sources from which it came, and thus allowing the reader to judge the possible bias of such sources. Finally, footnotes allow a writer to discuss interesting sidelights of the material without breaking the flow of writing:
Two questions invariably arise whenever footnotes are required:

1. What should be footnoted?
2. What form is correct, particularly if unusual or specialized material is being used, such as mimeographed campaign literature?

WHAT TO FOOTNOTE

While most style manuals or term paper handbooks deal with footnote form, few ever touch upon the more difficult and confusing question, such as "What kind of source should I footnote and how often should I do it?" There are no ready answers to this question and unfortunately it is quite easy to sucumb to excess in either direction. If one feels uneasy about an assignment, the material, or the professor's standards and expectations, it is quite tempting to "over-document" a paper or to hang footnotes on it as though one were decorating a Christmas tree. This approach can be quite hazardous, for besides wasting time, the reader is overburdened with needless side trips to the bottom of the page and the likelihood of making technical errors is increased. Such errors would, of course, detract from the substance of a paper. Unnecessary footnotes, far from being a safeguard, can become a real problem.

Equally hazardous is the practice of "under-documentation." If footnoting has always been a mystery, something to be avoided, the possibility arises that the material will be distorted: important points may be omitted in order to avoid documentation, or the source of information and ideas may be left to the reader's imagination, implying that the work of others is somehow your own. Between these two unfortunate extremes three styles of scholarship are defined: the original scholar, the scholarly summarizer, and the essayist and journalist. The style which most closely approximates the assigned type of paper should be followed. the *original scholar* form is appropriate for PhD dissertations, Masters theses, honors papers, or term papers which fulfill the major portion of the requirements of a course. This style should also be used for papers consisting mainly of scholarly research from primary sources.

The *scholarly summarizer* style is appropriate for more-frequently assigned term papers which fulfill a minor portion of the requirements for a course. This type of paper usually consists of a summary, interpretation, synthesis of secondary sources.

The *essayist and journalist* style is also appropriate for many types of term papers, but in such cases the emphasis is upon the writer's own experience or interpretation. Strictly speaking, there are few ideas which are completely new; however, if the emphasis is to be on an original and creative reaction to these ideas, and not the ideas themselves or their origin, the essayist style is appropriate. This style may also be used if the paper is primarily a personal account or a narrative of events witnessed or situations in which the writer participated.

Table 4 summarizes the use of footnotes for each of the styles of scholarship.

Quotations   There is little question concerning the footnoting of direct quotations. The original scholar and the scholarly summarizer almost always footnote direct quotations. The exception for even the most scholarly styles are quotations from such items of public domain as the Bible and The Constitution. In such cases it is permissable to incorporate a general reference into the text of the material.

EXAMPLE: There seemed little question that the proposal violated the "equal protection clause," the Fourteenth Amendment to the Constitution.
The dogmatic insistence of the neighborhood leader's position reminded one of Henry Clay's, "Sir, I would rather be right than President."

Form for quotations is covered in the next section.
The essayist and journalist make even greater use of the device of incorporating general references into the body of the text.

EXAMPLE: The writer as a witness or observer: "Sir Reynarid replied, 'We know that you will carry on. We would also if we saw any hope of victory.'" Winston S. Churchill, *Their Finest Hour, The Second World War* (Boston: Houghton Mifflin Co., 1949).

The original scholar footnotes all but the most obvious facts. If in doubt he asks himself if the average mature reader would automatically be aware of the origin and authenticity of a particular fact. If not, it should be footnoted. In general the three criteria for footnoting facts are:

1. *Controversiality*: Could honest men disagree over the authenticity or significance of this fact?
2. *Significance* to the paper: Does a significant part of your argument rest upon this fact?
3. *Obscurity*: Are the means or sources for establishing the authenticity of this fact beyond the average reader's experience or recall?

In general, if a fact could be questioned in a scholarly paper on the basis of any of these three criteria it should be footnoted.

The scholarly summarizer needs to footnote only a representative sampling of his significant facts. In this way, the type of sources used is indicated. Obscure facts need not be footnoted unless they are central to the significance of the paper.

The essayist and journalist seldom footnotes facts unless they are both controversial and significant to the basic purpose of the paper.

Commentary and Interpretation   Not every individual will read a report with the same interest. Some readers will be interested only in the main conclusions and the general thread of ideas while others will be interested in exploring in depth various aspects of the supporting evidence. Other readers will want to read the interesting sidelights found in research; some will find these sidelights a definite distraction. How is it possible for one manuscript to please such widely varying tastes?

Footnotes which comment upon and interpret data can be a partial solution to this dilemma. Such footnotes can be used for supplementary information which will be of interest to some readers. Again, the use of such footnotes varies with the style of scholarship. The original scholar does not want to overburden his text with a full explanation of the development of his methodology. In order to fully understand the methodology it is also important to make the scope of articles in journals or books dealing with this methodology available to the reader. Such an explanation takes the form of the bibliographical footnote.

EXAMPLE: Cf. Glendon Schubert, "Ideologies and Attitudes, Academic and Judicial," *Journal of Politics* 29 (February, 1967): 3-40; "Academic Ideology and the Study of Adjudication," *Saturday Review* 61 (March, 1967): 106-129; I. Howard, Jr., "On the Fluidity of Judical Choice," *American Political Science Review* 62 (May, 1968): 43.

If library rather than empirical research is used, a similar bibliographical footnote dealing with library sources is appropriate.

EXAMPLE: Prominent commentary on political obligations was offered by Thomas Aquinas, Locke, Rousseau, and notably T.H. Green, who may have been the first to use the term. A study of Green's thought and environment is Melvin Richter, *The Politics of Conscience*: *T.H. Green and His Age* (Cambridge: Harvard University

Table 4 Three types of scholarship and appropriate footnote use.

Type of Information	Original Scholar	Scholarly Summarizer	Essayist and Journalist
Quotations	All except those quotations of common knowledge, in which case they would still be footnoted if they varied from one edition to another.	Same as original scholar	Only if the quotation is controversial or highly significant to the text in which case the reference would be incorporated into the body of the material.
Facts 1. Controversial 2. Significant to the paper 3. Obscure	All but those which are part of common knowledge.	All controversial facts, a representative amount of significant facts to indicate the nature of sources, and only obscure facts which are central to the meaning of the paper.	Only controversial facts central to the meaning of the paper.

Commentary and Interpretation

Methodology	Brief bibliographical essay showing the scope of material.	Refers to other works which would contain bibliographical essays.	Only if different but similar methodology would yield significantly different results.
Context of opinions and sources	Brief bibliographical essay showing scope of material	Refers to other works which would contain bibliographical essays.	Only to indicate that the author is aware of major different approaches; can be incorporated into the text.
Tangential information	Used frequently for points which might need amplification.	Only for points the absence of which might distort the meaning of the work.	Rarely used except for humor.

Press, 1964), pp. 5-57. Also, review John Plamenatz, *Consent, Freedom, and Political Obligation*, 2nd. ed. (New York: Oxford University Press, 1968).

The original scholar also can use footnotes to provide tangential information, as in the following.

EXAMPLES: Information concerned with research methodology: "We exclude respondents who claimed knowledge but are unable to produce a fragment of an accurate observation." Raymond E. Wolfinger and Fres I. Greenstein, "The Repeal of Fair Housing in California," *The American Political Science Review* 62 (September, 1968): 955.

Meaning of words: "The Russian word for election, *vybory*, literally means choices, alternatives." Jerome M. Gilisin, "Soviet Elections as a Measure of Dissent: The Missing One Percent," *American Political Science Review* 62 (September, 1968): 85.

Clarifying Information: "It should be kept in mind that each Soviet voter casts several ballots — as many as seven — so that two million negative votes represent perhaps on the order of 500,000 to 700,000 dissenters." Jerome M. Gilisin, "Soviet Elections as a Measure of Dissent: The Missing One Percent," *American Political Science Review* 62 (September 1968): 816.

Where the original scholar uses footnotes to present a short bibliographical essay on his sources, the scholarly summarizer uses footnotes to point to the location of such documentation in other sources. This identification of other sources is equally useful for both library and empirical research.

EXAMPLES: Methodological: For a useful survey of different methods that have been used to analyze roll-call data, see Lee F. Anderson, Meredith W. Watts, Jr., and Allen R. Wilcox, *Legislative Roll-Call Analysis* (Evanston, Ill.: Northwestern University Press, (1966). See also Duncan MacRae, Jr.,

Issues and Parties in Legislative
Voting: Methods of Statistical Analysis (New York: Harper & Row, 1970)
for a careful and systematic review
of the statistical literature relevant
to roll-call analysis.

From Stephen J. Brams and Michael K. O'Leary "An Axiomatic
Model of Voting Bodies", *American Political Science Review*, 64,
p. 449, June 1970.

Library sources: P.W. Bridgmen is generally regarded as the
father of the operational philosophy, and his intel-
lectual indebtedness to Bentley is reflected in
Bridgman, "Error, Quantum Theory, and the
Observer," in Richard W. Taylor (ed.), *Life,
Language, Law: Essays in Honor of Arthur F.
Bentley* (Yellow Springs, Ohio: Antioch Press,
1957), pp. 125-131.

From Steven R. Brown and John Ellithorp, "Emotional Experiences in Political Groups: The Case of the McCarthy Phenomona",
American Political Science Review, 64, p. 349, June 1970.

Context of Opinions: For this position, see Richard Wasserstrom,
"Disobeying the Law," *The Journal of
Philosophy*, 58 (1961): 641-653. Also,
I. Howard, Jr. "On the Fluidity of Judicial
Choice", *The American Political Science
Review*, 62 (1968): 80.

The scholarly summarizer thus uses interpretative footnotes to
demonstrate that he is aware of the broader scope of material, but
does not feel compelled to list all of them himself.

The essayist and journalist is much more likely to incorporate
such comments and interpretations into his text. However, if the
essayist or journalist uses a research method, different versions
of which yield highly different results, he is also compelled to make
some justification of his methodology. Such justifications tend to
break the flow of writing and again they can be placed in footnotes.

EXAMPLE: "I rely for this version of the Vice-Presidential
selection on the excellent and exclusive reporting of
Carleton Kent, in the *Chicago Sun-Times*, reporting

acknowledged by those who were present to be authentic." Theodore H. White, *The Making of the President* New York: (Antheneum Press, 1961), pp. 201.

The same instructions apply to the use of library sources.

EXAMPLE: "One of the landmark studies in the field of business administration is *Strategy and Structure* by A.D. Chandler, Jr." Lawrence E. Fouraker and John M. Stopford, "Organization, Structure and the Multination Strategy," *Administrative Science Quarterly* 13 (1968): 485.

Some essayists also place tangential material in footnotes as a humorous literary device.

EXAMPLE: "'Where did you sleep last night and the night before that?' (This last is an essay question, for the air traveler is usually able to declare, in good faith, that he has not slept at all for the past week)." C. Northcote Parkinson, *Parkinson's Law and Other Studies in Administration* (Boston: Houghton Mifflin Co., 1957), p. 108.

FORM

Footnote and bibliography forms are one of the few things in life in which one can justifiably be arbitrary. There is no inherent reason to use one form rather than another, except for the sake of clear communication and consistency. The works used should be cited in the same form as that used in indexes, bibliographies, or library card catalogues. In this way, a reader will be able to locate cited sources.

Following are examples of the most frequent types of footnotes and bibliographies used in a political science paper, along with general comments and explanations. Most of the forms are based upon *The University of Chicago Manual of Style*, 12th ed., rev. (Chicago, Ill.: The University of Chicago Press, 1969). The Chicago manual does not specifically cover several forms such as interviews and political pamphlets, which are likely to be used by students of political science. In such cases, examples given are consistent with Kate L. Turabian, *Student Guide for Writing College*

Papers, 2nd ed. rev. (Chicago: The University of Chicago Press, 1969). The legal citations as based upon *A Uniform System of Citation*, 11th ed., *Harvard Law Review*, 1968.

BIBLIOGRAPHY

All three styles of scholarship utilize bibliographies, but there is a slight variation between the two more scholarly styles and the essayist of journalist. Both the original scholar and the scholarly summarizer place their bibliographic entries in catagories of written form. The most common are: books, periodicals, newspapers (sometimes combined with periodicals), government documents, dissertations, unpublished manuscripts, interviews, and letters. The essayist and journalist usually do not have enough citations to justify separate categories, and they simply list all of their sources alphabetically, by the last name of the author. A bibliography should include all works cited in footnotes plus any other works which were used. Works which were examined but not used should not be cited.

Footnotes, General Rules

Books Should Include
  1. Author's full name
  2. Complete title
  3. editor, compiler, or translator (if any)
  4. name of series, volume or series number (if any)
  5. number of volumes
  6. city, publisher, and date
  7. volume number and page number
Articles Should Include
  1. Author
  2. Title of article
  3. Periodical
  4. Volume of periodical
  5. Date and page numbers of article
Unpublished Material Should Include
  1. Author
  2. Title (if any)
  3. Type of material
  4. Where it may be found
  5. Date
  6. Page number (if any)

Bibliography, General Rules

Footnote style can be changed in bibliographic style by transposing author's first and last names, removing parenthesis from facts of publication, omitting page references, and repunctuating with periods instead of commas.

Books
1. Name of author(s), editors, or institutions responsible
2. Full title, including subtitle if one exists
3. Series, if any
4. Volume number
5. Editions, if not the original
6. Publisher's name (sometimes omitted)
7. Date of publication

Articles Should Include
1. Name of author
2. Title of article
3. Name of periodical
4. Volume number (or date, or both)
5. Pages

Book With One Author

Footnote: 2. George Sabine, *A History of Political Theory* (New York: Holt, Rinehart, & Winston, Inc., 1961), pp. 467-68.

Bibliography: Sabine, George. *A History of Political Theory.* New York: Holt, Rinehart, & Winston, Inc., 1961.

Comments: Titles of other works appearing in the title are in quotation marks.

Book With Two Authors

Footnote: 3. Robert Dahl and Charles Lindblom, *Politics, Economics, and Welfare* (New York: Harper & Row, Publishers, 1953), p. 115.

Bibliography: Dahl, Robert, and Lindblom, Charles. *Politics, Economics, and Welfare.* New York: Harper & Row, Publishers, 1953.

Book With Three Authors

Footnote: 4. John R. Meyer, John F. Kain, and Martin Wohl, *The Urban Transportation Problem* (Cambridge, Mass.: Harvard University Press, 1968), p. 50.

Bibliography: Meyer, John; Kain, John F.; and Wohl, Martin. *The Urban Transportation Problem.* Cambridge, Mass: Harvard University Press, 1968.

Book With More Than Three Authors

Footnote: 5. John Wahlke et al., *The Legislative System* (New York: John Wiley & Sons, Inc., 1962), p. 23.

Bibliography: Wahlke, John; Eulau, Heinz; Buchanan, William; and Ferguson, LeRoy C. *The Legislative System.* New York: John Wiley & Sons, Inc., 1962.

Book With An Association As Author

Footnote: 33. National Manpower Council, *Government and Manpower* (New York: Columbia University Press, 1964), p. 76.

Bibliography: National Manpower Council. *Government and Manpower.* New York: Columbia University Press, 1964.

Pseudonym, Author's Real Name Known

Footnote: 35. Samuel Clemens [Mark Twain]. *Huckleberry Finn.* (New York: Harcourt, Brace & World, 1969), p. 8.

Bibliography: Clemens, Samuel [Mark Twain]. *Huckleberry Finn.* New York: Harcourt, Brace & World, 1969.

Author's Name Not on Title Page, But Known

Footnote: 7. [Alexander Hamilton, James Madison, and John Jay], *The Federalist Papers*, ed. Jacob Cook (Middletown, Conn.: Wesleyan University Press, 1961), p. 182.

Bibliography: [Hamilton, Alexander; Madison, James; and Jay, John.] *The Federalist Papers.* Edited by Jacob

Cook. Middletown, Conn: Wesleyan University Press, 1961.

Book's Author Anonymous

Footnote: 6. *The Holy Quran*, (Washington, D.C.: Islamic Center, 1960), p. 177.

Bibliography: *The Holy Quran*. Washington, D.C.: Islamic Center, 1960.

Comments: Avoid use of "Anon." or "Anonymous."

Book By Editor, Compiler or Translator:
No Other Author Listed

Editors

Footnote: 8. Robert Theobold, ed., *Social Policies for America in the Seventies: Nine Divergent Views* (New York: Double-day & Co., Inc., 1968), p. 85.

Bibliography: Theobold, Robert, ed. *Social Policies for America in the Seventies: Nine Divergent Views.* New York: Doubleday & Co., Inc., 1968.

Compilers

Footnote: 9. Robert Lindsay and John Neu, comps., *French Political Pamphlets, 1547-1648* (Madison: University of Wisconsin Press, 1969), p. 8.

Bibliography: Lindsay, Robert, and Neu, John, comps. *French Political Pamphlets, 1547-1684.* Madison: University of Wisconsin Press, 1969.

Translators

Footnote: 10. Ursule Molinaro, trans., *Beowolf* (New York: Farrar, Straus, & Giroux, Inc., 1957), p. 23.

Bibliography: Molinaro, Ursule, trans. *Beowolf.* New York: Farra, Straus, & Giroux, Inc., 1957.

Translated or Edited Books in Which the Author
is Known

Footnote: 20. Gustav Stolper, Karl Hauser, and Knut Borchardt, *The German Economy 1870 to Present,* trans. Toni Stoper (New York: Harcourt, Brace & World, 1969), pp. 8-10.

Bibliography: Stolper, Gustav; Hauser, Karl; and Borchardt, Knut. *The German Economy 1870 to Present*. Translated by Toni Stoper. New York: Harcourt, Brace, & World, 1969.

Edited or Translated Work in Which the Editor is More Important than the Author

Footnote: 11. William L. Riordon, ed. *Plunkitt of Tammany Hall*, by George Washington Plunkitt (New York: E.P. Dutton & Co., 1900), p. 25.

Bibliography: Riordon, William L., ed. *Plunkitt of Tammany Hall,* by George Washington Plunkitt. New York: E.P. Dutton & Co., Inc., 1900.

Books, Multivolume

Footnote: 23. Fred E. Inbau, James R. Thompson, and Cladue R. Sowle, *Cases and Comments on Criminal Justice*, 3 vols. (Mineloa, N.Y.: The Foundation Press, Inc., 1968), 1:5.

Bibliography: Inbau, Fred E.; Thompson, James R.; Sowle, Cladue R. *Cases and Comments on Criminal Justice*. Vol. 1. Mineloa, N.Y.: The Foundation Press, Inc., 1968.

Book in a Series

Footnote: 2. W. F. Gutteridge, *The Military in African Politics*, Studies in African History (London: Methuen & Co. Ltd., 1969), p. 22.

Bibliography: Gutteridge, W. F. *The Military in African Politics*. Studies in African History. London: Methuen & Co. Ltd., 1969.

Comments: If a book is part of a series the citations should include the name of the series and the volume number. Spell out the author's name in full unless he is commonly known by his initials, e.g., W. F. Gutteridge.

Book in a Series, One Author, Several Volumes, Each With a Different Title

Footnote: 36. Charles Edward Mallet, *The Medieval University and Colleges Founded in the Middle Ages*, 3 vols., The

History of Oxford University (New York: Barnes & Noble, Inc., 1968), 1:23.

Bibliography: Mallet, Charles Edward. *The Medieval University and Colleges Founded in the Middle Ages.* Vol 1. The History of Oxford University. New York: Barnes & Noble, Inc., 1968.

Paperback Edition of a Book
First Published in Hard Cover

Footnote: 22. Aaron Wildavsky, *The Politics of the Budgetary Process* (Boston: Little, Brown and Co., paperback, 1964), p. 177.

Bibliography: Wildavsky, Aaron. *The Politics of the Budgetary Process.* Paperback. Boston: Little, Brown and Co., 1964.

Introduction to Book by Another Author

Footnote: 34. Alex Inkeles, Introduction to *The Process of Modernization,* by John Brode (Cambridge: Harvard University Press, 1969), p. vii.

Bibliography: Inkeles, Alex. Introduction to *The Process of Modernization*, by John Brode. Cambridge: Harvard University Press, 1969.

Citation in One Book from Another Book

Footnote: 42. Jakob Hegemann, *Entlarvte Geschichte*, p. 210. As quoted in John W. Wheeler-Bennett's, *The Nemesis of Power* (London: MacMillan & Co., Ltd., 1954), p. 8.

Bibliography: Wheeler-Bennett, John W. *The Nemesis of Power.* London: MacMillan & Co. Ltd., 1954.

Book Review

Footnote: 38. Willard Ranger, "International Politics, Law, and Organization," Review of *Regionalism and World Order*, by Ronald Yalem, *The American Political Science Review* 60 (September, 1966): 759.

Bibliography: Ranger, Willard. "International Politics, Law, and Organization." Review of *Regionalism and World*

Order by Ronald Yalem. *The American Political Science Review* 60 (September, 1966): 759.

Literature

Plays and Long Poems

Footnote: 57. George Barnard Shaw, *The Devil's Advocate*, act 2, sc.1, lines 8-11.

Bibliography: Shaw, George Barnard. *The Devil's Advocate.*

Short Poems

Footnote: 58. Edgar Allen Poe, "To Helen," *Eternal Passion in English Poetry* (Freeport, N.Y.: Books for Libraries, Inc., 1969), lines 3-5.

Bibliography: Poe, Edgar Allen. "To Helen." *Eternal Passion in English Poetry.* Freeport, N.Y.: Books for Libraries, Inc., 1969.

Bible

Footnote: 14.1 Ruth 12:18.

Bibliography: 1. *Book of Ruth* 12:18.

Classical Works

Footnote: 15. Julius Ceasar *The Conquest of Gaul* 1., 3-5.

Bibliography: Ceasar, Julius. *The Conquest of Gaul* 1.

Modern Edition of Classical Work

Footnote: 4. Augustine, *City of God,* trans. Healey-Tasker 20.3.

Bibliography: Augustine. *City of God.* Translated by Healey-Tasker.

Article, Chapter, or Other Part of a Book

Footnote: 16. Leonard D. White, "The Role of the City Manager," *Urban Government*, rev. ed., edited by Edward C. Banfield (New York: The Free Press, 1969), p. 286.

Bibliography: White, Leonard D. "The Role of the City Manager."

Urban Government, rev. ed., edited by Edward C. Banfield. New York: The Free Press, 1969.

Works Available in Microfilm

Footnote: 18. Abraham Tauber, *Spelling Reform in the United States*, (Ann Arbor, Mich.: University Microfilms, 1958.

Bibliography: Tauber, Abraham. *Spelling Reform in the United States*. Ann Arbor, Mich.: University Microfilms, 1958.

Encyclopedias, Almanacs, and Other Reference Works

Signed Articles
Footnote: 24. *International Encyclopedia, of the Social Sciences*, 5th ed., s.v. "Systems Analysis: Political Systems," by William C. Mitchell.

Bibliography: *International Encyclopedia of the Social Sciences*, 5th ed., s.v. "Systems Analysis: Political Science, by William C. Mitchell.

Unsigned Articles
Footnote: 25. *Oxford Dictionary of National Biography*, s.v. "Akers-Douglas, Aretas."

Bibliography: *Oxford Dictionary of National Biography.* s.v. "Akers-Douglas, Aretas."

Periodical: Author Given

Consecutive Pages
Footnote: 32. David Fellman, "Constitutional Law in 1958-1959," *American Political Science Review* 54 (1960): 168-70.

Bibliography: Fellman, David. "Constitutional Law in 1958-1959." *American Political Science Review* 54 (1960): 168-70.

Nonconsecutive Pages
Footnote: 33. Will Lissner, "Protection of the Author's Reprint Rights," *American Journal of Economics* 28 (April, 1969): 211.

Bibliography: Lissner, Will. "Protection of the Author's Reprint Rights." *American Journal of Economics* 28 (April, 1968): 211.

Magazine Article, No Author Given

Footnote: 39. "Tax Changes for 1971: The Plans Take Shape,"
U.S. News & World Reports, 5 October 1970, p. 91.

Bibliography: "Tax Changes for 1971: The Plans Take Shape."
U.S. News & World Reports, 5 October 1970,
p. 91.

Newspapers

American
Footnote: 12. George C. Wilson, "Copter Force Hits Camp Near
Hanoi," *The Washington Post*, 24 November 1970, p. 1A.

Bibliography: Wilson, George C, "Copter Force Hits Camp Near
Hanoi," *The Washington Post* Vol. 351. 24
November 1970. p. 1A and 14A.

Foreign
Footnote: 13. *Times* (London), 1 December 1970, p. 10.

Bibliography: *Times.* London. 1 December 1970. p. 10.

Comments: Include name of city for foreign newspapers.

Proceedings of a Meeting or Conference: Reproduced

Footnote: 23. The Seventy-seventh Annual Conference of the International Chiefs of Police, "Proceedings of the Conference
of the International Chiefs of Police," mimeographed
(Atlantic City: C.I.C.P., October 6, 1970, p. 2.

Bibliography: The Seventy-seventh Annual Conference of the Inter-
national Chiefs of Police. "Proceedings of the
International Chiefs of Police." Atlantic City:
C.I.C.P. October 6, 1970.

Minutes of a Meeting: Not Reproduced

Footnote: 69. Capitol Improvement Advisory Committee, "Minutes of
Meeting of Capitol Improvement Advisory Committee,"
(Washington, D.C., 5 May 1971), p. 2.

Bibliography: Capitol Improvement Advisory Committee. "Minutes
of Meeting of Capitol Improvement Advisory Committee." Washington, D.C., 5 May 1971.

Paper Read or Speech Delivered at a Meeting

Footnote: 12. John N. Mitchell, "Legalized Wiretapping" (Address delivered at the Seventy-seventh Annual Conference of the International Chiefs of Police, Atlantic City, October 5, 1970), p. 5.

Bibliography: Mitchell, John N. "Legalized Wiretapping." Paper read at the seventy-seventh Annual Conference of International Chiefs of Police, October 5, 1970, at Atlantic City, N.J. Mimeographed.

Thesis or Dissertation

Footnote: 25. William John Thomson, "Variables Affecting Human Discrimination Processes," (Ph.D. dissertation, Stanford University, 1969), p. 87.

Bibliography: Thomson, William John. "Variables Affecting Human Discrimination Processes." Ph.D. dissertation, Stanford University, 1969.

Legal Citations

Federal Statute
Footnote: 26. *Administrative Procedure Act,* @ 11-6 U.S.C.@1009 (1964).

Bibliography: *Administrative Procedure Act.*@11-6 U.S.C.@1009 (1964).

State Statute
Footnote: 27. *Blue Sky Law.*@2 New York General Business Code @ 352, (McKinney, 1962).

Bibliography: *Blue Sky Law.*@2 New York General Business Code@352, McKinney, 1962.

Court Case
Footnote: 28. Ker v. California, 357 U.S. 50. (1963).

Bibliography: Ker v. California. 357 U.S. 50 (1963).

Law Review Articles
Footnote: 29. Ebb, *The Grundig-Consten Case Revisited,* 115 UNIV. PENN. L. REV., 885 (1969).

Bibliography: Ebb. *The Grundig-Consten Case Revisited.* 115 UNIV. PENN. L. REV., 1969.

Statutory Material

Footnote: 30. U.S., *Constitution,* Art. 2, sec. 1.

Bibliography: U.S. *Constitution*, Art. 2, sec. 1.

Material from Manuscript Collections

Footnote: 31. Diary of Lewis Tappan, 23 February 1836 to 29 August 1838, Tappan Papers, Library of Congress, Washington, D.C.

Bibliography: Washington, D.C. Library of Congress. Diary of Lewis Tappan. Tappan Papers 25 Fedbruary 1836 to 29 August 1838.

Radio and Television Programs

Footnote: 40. C.B.S., *C.B.S. Evening News*, 8 December 1970, "Rube Goldberg Dies," Walter Cronkite, reporter.

Bibliography: C.B.S. *C.B.S. Evening News.* 8 December 1970. "Rube Goldberg Dies." Walter Cronkite, reporter.

Interview

Footnote: 41. Interview with Mr. Carl Rauh, Deputy Attorney General for the District of Columbia, Washington, December 2, 1970.

Bibliography: Interview with Mr. Carl Rauh. Deputy Attorney General for the District of Columbia. Washington. December 2, 1970.

Mimeographed or Other Nonprinted Reports

Footnote: 13. American University, "Codebook: Baker Survey of Local Elected Officials," mimeographed (Washington: American University School of Government), p. 5.

Bibliography: American University. "Codebook: Baker Survey of Local Elected Officials." Washington: American University School of Government.

Pamphlet

Footnote: 59. Harold T. Effer, "Joseph Clark, Your Man in Washington," Office of Sen. Clark (Washington, D.C., Fall, 1968), p. 2.

Bibliography: Effer, Harold T. "Joseph Clark, Your Man in Washington." Office of Sen. Clark. Washington, D.C.,
Fall, 1970.

Letters

Footnote: 68. Lawrence to Barr, 8 November 1958, Political Papers
of Governor David Leo Lawrence, Hillman Library
University of Pittsburgh, Pittsburgh, Pa.

Bibliography: Pittsburgh, Pa. Hillman Library University of
Pittsburgh. Political Papers of Governor David
Leo Lawrence. Lawrence to Barr, 8 November
1958.

Documents

Citing documents is always a difficult problem, for their form
is totally unlike that of books and magazines. The card catalogue is
a good guide and the following general rules should help. Include in
this order:

1. The country (U.S. etc.)
2. Branch of Government (Legislative executive, etc.)
3. The subbranch or subbranches (House, Committee on Education and Labor, etc.)

The branches of subbranches can become complicated: a careful examination of the document itself, its entry is the card catalogue,
or the *Government Organization Manual* (see page 000) should
give you an idea as to the sequence of organization.

This information is followed by the title (underlined), the name
of the series or sequence, and the facts of publication. The following
examples include the most commonly cited government publications.

Congressional Documents

Bills
Footnote: 45. U.S., Congress, House, *Higher Education Act of
1965*, H.R. 9567, 89th Cong., 1st sess. 1965, p. 37.

Bibliography: U.S. Congress. House. *Higher Education Act of
1965*. H.R. 9567, 89th Cong., 1st sess., 1965.

Footnote: 46. U.S., Congress, Senate, *Metropolitian Planning Act*, S. 855, 88th Cong., 2nd sess., 1964.

Bibliography: U.S. Congress. Senate. *Metropolitan Planning Act.* S. 885, 88th Cong., 2nd sess., 1964.

Debates
Footnotes: 47. U.S., Congress, Senate, *Congressional Record*, 91st Cong., 2nd sess, 1970. 25, pt. S11: 665.

Bibliography: U.S. Congress. Senate. *Congressional Record.* 91st Congress, 2nd sess., 1970. 25, pt. 511: 665.

Report
Footnote: 48. U.S., Congress, House, *Higher Education Act of 1965*, H. Rept. 621 to accompany H.R. 9567, 89th Cong., 1st sess., 1965.

Bibliography: U.S. Congress. House. *Higher Education Act of 1965.* H.R. 9567. 89th Cong., 1st sess., 1965.

Hearings
Footnote: 49. U.S., Congress, House, Committee on Ways and Means, Hearings to exclude from the gross income the first $750 of interest received on deposit in thrift institutions, H.R. 16545, 91st Cong., 2nd sess., 1970.

Bibliography: U.S. Congress. House. Committee on Ways and Means. Hearings to exclude from the gross income the first $750 of interest received on deposit in thrift institutions. H.R. 16545, 91st Cong. 2nd sess. 1970.

Executive Documents

From an Executive Department
Footnote: 43. U.S., Department of Interior, *Final Report to the President on the Potomac Basin: "The Nation's River"* (Washington, D.C.: U.S. Dept. of Interior, 1968), p. 6.

Bibliography: U.S. Department of Interior. *Final Report to the President on the Potomac Basin: "The Nation's River."* Washington D.C.: U.S. Dept. of Interior, 1968.

Presidential Papers
Footnote: 44. U.S., President, "Statement by the President on Actions and Recommendations for the Federal City, January 31,

1969," *Weekly Compilation of Presidential Documents* vol. 5, no. 5, February 3, 1970, p. 198.

Bibliography: U.S. President. "Statement by the President on Actions and Recommendations for the Federal City, January 31, 1969." *Weekly Compilation of Presidential Documents* 5. February 3, 1970.

International Documents

International Organizations

Footnote: 49. League of Nations, Secretariat, *Administration of Territory* (O.J.) (March, 1920), p. 52.

Bibliography: League of Nations. Secretariat. *Administration of Territory* (O.J.) (March, 1920).

Footnote: 50. United Nations, Economic and Social Council 54 Session, *Convention and Proticol for the Protection of Cultural Property in Event of Armed Conflict* (E/CL 1374) 7 July 1959, p. 2.

Bibliography: United Nations. Economic and Social Council, 54 Session. *Convention and Proticol for the Protection of Cultural Property in Event of a Armed Conflict.* (E/CL 1374) 7 July 1959.

Footnote: 51. United Nations, General Assembly, November 20, 1959, *General Assembly Resolution 1386*, A/4353, Annex 16, pp. 19-21.

Bibliography: United Nations. General Assembly. 14th Session, November 20, 1959. *General Assembly Resolution 1386*, A/4353.

Treaties

Footnote: 52. U.S., *Statutes at Large* 43, pt. 2 (December 1923-March 1925), "Naval Armament Limitation Treaty," February 26, 1922, ch. 1, art. 1, p. 1655.

Bibliography: U.S. *Statutes at Large* 43, pt. 2 (December 1923-March 1925). "Naval Arms Limitation Treaty," February 26, 1933.

State and Local Documents

State

Footnote: 57. New Jersey, Office of the Governor, Governor's Select

Commission on Civil Disorder, *Report for Action*, (Trenton: Office of the Governor, 1968), p. 14.

Bibliography: New Jersey. Office of the Governor. Governor's Select Commission on Civil Disorder. *Report for Action.* Trenton: Office of the Governor, 1968.

City

Footnote: 58. New York, N.Y., Mayor's Office, Mayor's Task Force on Reorganization of New York City Government. *The Mayor's Task Force on Reorganization of New York City Government: Report and Proposed Local Law*, (New York: Institute of Public Administration, 1966), p. 9.

Bibliography: New York, N.Y. Mayor's Office. Mayor's Task Force on Reorganization of New York City Government. *The Mayor's Task Force on Reorganization of New York City Government: Report and Proposed Local Law.* New York: Institute of Public Administration, 1966.

Second or Later References to Footnotes

Chances are several references will be made to the same footnote. The general rules are as follows:

1. For references to the same work with no intervening footnotes simply use the Latin term *"Ibid.,"* meaning in the same place.

2. For second references with no intervening footnote, but with a different page of the same work, state *Ibid.* and the page number.

EXAMPLE: *Ibid.*, p. 87.

3. For second references with intervening footnotes state: the author's last name, but not first name or initials unless another author of the same last name is cited; a shortened title of the work and the specific page number.

Following are examples of second citations of a representative number of works.

Second References with Intervening Citations

Book, Single Volume

First Citation: 1. Thomas E, Skidmore, *Politics in Brazil* (New York: Oxford University Press, Inc., 1967, p. 81.

Second Citation: 8. Thomas E. Skidmore, *Politics Brazil*, p. 92.

Multivolume
First Citation: 2. Fred E. Inbau, James R. Thomas, and Cladue R. Sowle, *Cases and Comments on Criminal Justice,* 3 vols., (Mineloa, N.Y.: The Foundation Press, Inc. 1968) 1:5.

Second Citation: 9. Inbau, Thomas, and Sowle, 1:8.

Article in Anthology
First Citation: 3. Ronald Cohen, "Anthropology and Political Science: Courtship and Marriage?" *Politics and the Social Sciences,* Seymour M. Lipset ed., (New York: Oxford University Press, Inc., 1969), p. 22.

Second Citation: 10. Cohen, "Anthropology and Political Science," p. 23.

Comment: More than one work by Cohen is cited thus shortened title is included.

Journal Article
First Citation: 4. David Fellman, "Constitutional Law in 1958-1959," *American Political Science Review* 54 (1960): 168.

Second Citation: 11. Fellman, p. 171.

Book with an Editor or Translator, Author Unknown
First Citation: 5. Robert Theobold, ed., *Social Policies for America in the Seventies: Nine Divergent Views* (Garden City, N.Y.: Doubleday & Co., Inc., 1968), p. 3.

Second Citation: 12. Robert Theobold, ed., *Social Policies in Seventies*, p. 4.

Classical
First Citation: 6. Thucydides, *History of the Peloponnesian Wars*, 2.30, 2.

Second Citation: 13. Thucy., 2.28, 1-6.

Letters
First Citation: 7. Stevens to Sumner, 28 August 1865, Charles Sumner Papers, Harvard College Library, Cambridge, Mass.

Second Citation: 14. Stevens to Sumner, 26 August 1865.

State Documents
First Citation: 15. Maryland, *Ordinance Number 438*, (1965) sec.
8.

Second Citation: 17. Maryland, *Ordinance Number 438*, sec. 8.

Federal Document
First Citation: 16. U.S., *Statutes at Large* 43, pt. 2 (Dec. 1923-
March 1925), "Naval Arms Limitation Treaty,"
Feb. 26, 1922, ch. 1, art. 1 p. 1655.

Second Citation: 18. U.S., *Statutes at Large* 43, "Naval Arms
Treaty", p. 1657.

PART II

Annotated Listing of Basic References

ABS Guide to Recent Publications in the Social and Behavioral Sciences. New York: The American Behavioral Scientist, Sage Publications, Inc. 1965 —.

Drawing from sociology, anthropology and psychology, the study of political science connects the older humanities-oriented studies (such as constitutional law and political philosophy) with the newer studies which measure the many aspects of human behavior. If one is interested in the psychological reasons behind a particular voting trend, for instance, this guide will be of service.

Advance Bibliography of Contents: Political Science and Government. Santa Barbara, Calif.: American Bibliographical Center, Cleo Press, 1969.

A new publication begun in 1969, this bibliography is issued eight times a year and contains the itemized contents of roughly 260 important journals. This bibliography provides an excellent opportunity to view the most current articles in the field at a glance. The June and December issues contain an accumulated author index, and the December issue holds an accumulated subject index for the past year.

America Votes. Pittsburgh: University of Pittsburgh Press, 1954 —.

This is a prodigious biennial collection of voting statistics; it covers all of the national elections from 1954 to the present, state by state. The detailed vote breakdown includes national, state, and county election statistics. State and county figures include total vote — Republican, Democratic, and splinter parties. Each national table is followed by a brief listing of the candidates and their national vote with an identification of the character- istics of the state vote. Special aspects of the Electoral College vote are included, and any variations between the plurality figures in these national tables and the Republican-Democratic plurality figures in the state sections are listed. Each state data section is followed by notes giving the composition of the vote in detail and indicating any special circumstances of the state vote — canvassing problems, organization of new counties, dual elector tickets, and so forth.

The major sources for the first volume of this collection are the two pioneer research studies of Edgar Eugene Robinson, *The Presidential Vote, 1896-1932* (Stanford, Calif.: Stanford University Press, 1934), and *They Voted for Roosevelt: The Presidential Vote, 1932-1944* (Stanford, Calif.: Stanford University Press, 1947).

American Agencies Interested in International Affairs. 5th ed. The Council on Foreign Relations. New York: Fredrick Praeger, 1964 —.

This guide to several hundred organizations based in the United States covers their purpose, organization, finance and activities (e. g., the Japan Society offers generally neutral information; the Committee of One Million, on the other hand, has a quite sharply limited target area against the admission of Communist China to the U. N.).

American Foreign Policy: Current Documents. Historical Office of the Bureau of Public Affairs. Washington, D. C.: Government Printing Office. 1941 —.

This is a yearly publication that gathers the more important messages, declarations, treaties, etc., which have surfaced during the year.

Almanac of Current World Leaders. Los Angeles, Calif.: 1959 —.

Those world leaders in the current news are fitted with brief biographies. Special note is taken of those national states in which leadership has changed since the last publication (which is quarterly), plus listing by nation of heads of state, cabinet ministers and their political affiliations. Also included is a chronological listing of events involving changes in governmental and other important posts.

The Annual Register of World Events. New York: St. Martins Press, 1758 —.

A British publication heavily emphasizing Great Britain and the Commonwealth in what is considered to be one of the best summaries of year-by-year events. It also covers such areas as political, economic and cultural events and speeches from around the world, with summaries. The events — political and nonpolitical — are written in notable prose and are integrated into quarterly reports.

Biography Index. New York: H. W. Wilson Co. 1947 —.

This quarterly with cumulations is the key index to biographical material. It includes all of the biographical references found in other indexes plus selected foreign references. Entries are arranged alphabetically with a subject index in the back of each issue. This subject index is especially helpful in attempting to identify important individuals in a particular field who are receiving public attention.

Book of the States. Chicago: Council of State Governments, 1935 —.

This biennial is a rich source of authoritative information on the actual structure, working methods, functioning, and financing of state governments. The legislative, executive, and judicial branches are outlined in depth according to their intergovernmental relations and the major areas of public service performed by each. The 1968-1969 edition has two supplements, which list the state officials and legislators.

Important statistics are also contained in these volumes: salaries and compensations of state legislators, divorce laws, voting laws and regulations, state departments, welfare budgets and payments, and educational salaries and budgets.

Book Review Digest. New York: H. W. Wilson Co., 1905 —.

This monthly publication is an indexed reference to selected book reviews drawn from about seventy-five English and American periodicals. It is arranged by title, and has title and subject indexes. Each issue covers from 300 to 400 titles. Excerpts from several reviews and a bibliography are presented for each book.

Book Review Index. Detroit: Gale Research Co., 1965—.

To a great extent, this monthly review with quarterly cumulations supplements the *Book Review Digest.* The index lists current book reviews in the social and natural sciences, although no excerpts of reviews are given, and there is only an author index.

Canadian News Facts: The Indexed Digest of Canadian Current Events. B. Martland and Stephen D. Pepper, eds. Toronto, Ontario: Marpep Publishing Ltd., 1967 —.

This digest is a twice-monthly publication that does in-depth wrapups on general news developments in the provincial capitals. It also covers foreign relations.

Comparative International Almanac. Morris L. Ernst and Judith A. Posner, eds. New York: The Macmillan Co., 1967—.

This almanac is an excellent source of comparative (as opposed to raw) data about nations. It contains information in the form of rates, ratios, estimates and comparisons as well as such particular items as suicide rates, phones per 1,000 population, life expectancies, and literacy rates. Organization is based on a country-by-country format plus a topical country-by-country ranking.

Congressional Digest. Washington, D. C.: Congressional Digest Corporation, 1921 —.

This privately printed monthly publication explores both sides of current controversial topics. After an opening state-ment of the question under discussion, pro and con arguments drawn from the opinions of world experts in that particular field are advanced. In the October 1965 issue, for instance, the question under debate is "Should Congress modify the 'Mallory Rule' of procedure in criminal cases?" The pro arguments are quoted from a congressional committee report of the majority; the con arguments, from the minority report of the same committee.

Congressional Directory. Washington, D. C.: Government Print-ing Office, 1809 —.

This directory, which appears with every session of Congress, contains information on United States congressmen. Each congressman is given a limited number of free copies to distribute to his constituents. The directory contains short biographical sketches of every member of both houses. It also lists the membership of each congressional committee and outlines the committee assignments given each member. One may locate herein the name of his congressman, a brief sketch of his life, and the boundaries of the voting district in which he lives. Further, information is furnished concerning his outcome in the last several elections.

The major executives of every government agency are also listed, as are members of the diplomatic corps and members of the press who have accredited seating in the congressional press galleries. A pocket edition of this directory contains a photograph of each member of Congress, but omits other information.

Congressional District Data Book and Supplements, Redistricted States. Washington, D. C.: Government Printing Office, 1961 —.

The particular value of this biennial supplement to the *Statistical Abstract of the United States* is that it contains a variety of statistical information that is either unavailable elsewhere or available only from a variety of sources. The book organizes this information by congressional district, making it possible to examine congressional voting in terms of the characteristics of each district. It includes items on vital statistics, bank deposits, retail trade, local governments, elections, housing, nonwhite population, and so forth.

Congressional Information Service Index to Publications of the United States Congress. Washington, D.C.: James B. Adler, 1970—.

Congressional documents contain extensive information on almost every important area of public policy, but often a day report is barred in a hearing or committee print. Without some sort of in-depth indexing such as this publication, these reports would be lost to the researcher.

The *CIS Index* has become, in its brief existence, a basic guide to information contained in the working papers of Congress. It is used not only to find the information needed, but also to provide the researcher with copies (microfiche or hard copies) of the documents. It covers the entire range of congressional publications, which is to say 400,000 pages a year of hearings, committee prints, House and Senate reports and other congressional documents.

Congressional Quarterly Service

Although privately printed since 1945 the "CQ" series of publications has achieved the status of an official publication and is the most frequently cited source of congressional information. Its major attribute is its concise factual arrangement of material previously tucked away in bulky government documents.

The Congressional Quarterly publications present a careful review of each session of Congress in both legislative and political areas. Facts, figures and unbiased commentary on all aspects of congressional activity are presented, including committee meetings and floor action. The president's position on all major legislation and rollcall votes in Congress are superimposed. Also included are the president's messages to Congress, his news conferences, his vetoes, and so on.

The basic publication of the service is the *Congressional Quarterly Weekly Report*. From this report a yearly *Congressional Quarterly Almanac* is compiled.

Congress and the Nation is a hard-bound volume documenting all major congressional and presidential actions and national political campaigns for the twenty-year period from 1945 to 1964. Volume II, covering the Johnson years (1965-1968), was published in 1969.

Congressional Quarterly also publishes semiannually a current handbook for the study of American government, the *Congressional Quarterly Guide to Current American Government*, which contains research material written and arranged for classroom and study use, as well as the *Editorial Research Reports*, a weekly publication that objectively assembles the facts involved in current controversial topics in well-researched and documented articles of about 6,000 words each. A library subscribing to the *Congressional Quarterly Weekly Report* probably also receives the *Editorial Research Reports*.

Congressional Record. Washington, D.C.: Government Printing Office, 1873—.

The *Record* is a nearly verbatim account of everything uttered aloud on the floor of Congress as well as of some material not actually spoken but entered as an "extension of remarks." It is published Monday through Friday as long as Congress is in session. The *Congressional Record* is a valuable source because congressmen frequently insert letters and articles that are in themselves primary sources of information on topics under discussion.

Prior to 1873 the *Congressional Record* was titled *Congressional Globe* (1833-1873); before that it was called *The Register of Debates* (1824-1837); and even earlier, *Annals of Congress* (1789-1824). It is cataloged under these titles in libraries. Each set consists of fifteen to twenty parts a year, including a separate index. In 1947 the *Daily Digest* volumes were added, which review highlights, list scheduled hearings of Congress, and summarize day-to-day committee activity.

The *Congressional Record* contains a two-part index, consisting of an alphabetical listing of subjects and names and a history of bills and resolutions arranged by their numbers. This second section is thought to be the best available source for tracing the route of a particular bill. Because this is a daily record, the best method of locating information is first to establish the date on which the debate took place.

A student may request his congressman to put his name on the mailing list for the *Congressional Record*. It is a free service rendered by congressmen to their constituents. However, unless the student is willing to read and digest some 200 pages a day, this would be wasteful, as each congressman is limited to sixty-four such free subscriptions. (For a fact sheet on the *Congressional Record* turn to p. 115.)

Congressional Serial Set. Washington, D. C.: Government Printing Office, 1817 —.

This set of 13,500 volumes is a collection of documents containing House and Senate journals, documents, and reports. It does not include bills, hearings, laws, or "committee prints." The reports are committee reports and are especially important in that they contain not only brief summaries of the hearings but also the individual views of the committee members who participated. Committee reports usually contain the best brief summary of all the important facts and arguments related to the bill in question.

Obviously, it can be difficult to trace a document through 13,500 volumes, so the following indexes, all published by the Government Printing Office, can help one find a particular item.

Checklist of United States Public Documents, 1789-1909.
(Washington, D.C.: Government Printing Office, 1911.
Reprinted, New York: Kraus Reprint Co., 1962).
Catalog of the Public Documents of Congress, 1893-1940.
(Washington, D.C.: Government Printing Office). Pub-
pished irregularly between 1896 and 1945.
Decennial Cumulative Index 1941-1950. 25 vols. (Wash-
ington, D.C.: Government Printing Office, 1953). Suc-
ceeded by an index series published yearly, *Numerical
Lists and Schedules of Volumes of the Reports and
Documents* for each session of Congress. First pub-
lished for the seventy-third Congress (1933-1934), published biennially thereafter.

*The Monthly Catalog of United States Government Publica-
tions* lists each volume as it is sent to the depository libraries,
and is, itself, sent to each library as an index. These "depository libraries" are usually the state universities in the larger
cities of every state.

*The Constitution of the United States of America-Analysis
and Interpretation.* The Legislative Reference Service of the
Library of Congress of the United States. Washington, D. C.:
Government Printing Office, 1964.

This is a definitive work on the United States Constitution.
Article by article, amendment by amendment, this authoritative
work summarizes the leading cases that have shaped the interpretation of the Constitution. For example, if one wishes to know
exactly what is meant by the "right to a speedy and public
trial," he can find in this book a concise summary of applicable
cases. The sole drawback of this book is its date of publication,
since important decisions after 1964 are not included.

Council of Social Science Data Archives. Pittsburgh, Pa.:
University of Pittsburgh Press, 1965 —.

This publication coordinates the projects of nearly every
data archive in the nation and in Canada. It distributes to members
information on the accessibility of particular survey data in
the U. S. and abroad. The CSSDA invites queries from students
regarding the location of data in the social sciences.

County and City Data Book. Washington, D.C.: Government
Printing Office, 1952—.

This study has been published annually since 1965; earlier editions covered staggered time periods from 1949 to 1953. It is basically a supplement to the *Statistical Abstract of the United States*, combining two separate earlier publications, *Cities Supplement* (1944) and *County Data Book* (1947). It covers 144 items for each county in the United States and 148 items for each of the 683 cities having 25,000 or more inhabitants. Items for counties include population, dwelling units, retail trade, wholesale trade, selected service trades, manufacturers, vital statistics, and agriculture units. For city units, government, finances, school systems, hospitals, and climate are added. It also contains this same information for geographic regions and divisions, for states, and for standard metropolitan areas. Descriptive text and source notes are included.

Cumulative Book Index. New York: H. W. Wilson Co., 1898 —.

This monthly index with compilations provides a comprehensive list of the books published in various areas of interest, some of which might not be found in a college library. It supplies a list of publications as they come off the presses and usually lists the other works of each author. Also of value to the researcher is a selected list of important government documents, which is included in the index. Since 1925 the *Cumulative Book Index* has included books in the English language that are published outside the United States.

Current Biography. New York: H. W. Wilson Co., 1940 —.

Current Biography supplies unbiased, well-written sketches of contemporary personalities in about forty different professional fields. It contains photographs of each subject, gives the proper pronunciation of the more difficult names, and lists references to additional material. Each issue contains an accrued list index of the previous issues. Besides the annual compilation, there are ten-year indexes.

Current Digest of the Soviet Press. The American Association for the Advancement of Slavic Studies. Columbus, Ohio: Ohio State University Press, 1929 —.

Next to being there, this publication is considered one of the best ways to study the Soviet Union. Each week it publishes American translations of all the major documents and significant articles from about sixty Soviet newspapers and magazines plus a complete index to the two principal dailies,

Pravda and *Izvestia*. The translations are without comment or even interpretation but are, rather, excellent raw material for critical analysis done under the watchful eye of an experienced teacher. A detailed quarterly index is also published as is a new monthly, *Current Abstracts of the Soviet Press*, offering, obviously, the monthly highlights of Soviet news with emphasis on internal discussion.

Daily Report. Washington, D.C.: The Foreign Broadcast
Information Service, 1947 —.
    Not everything the CIA does is secret. This governmental source is a verbatum report of the CIA's monitoring of news broadcasts of dozens of countries, with emphasis upon the Soviet Union, Communist China and other Communist satellites.

Deadline Data on World Affairs. Greenwich, Conn.: Deadline
Data, Inc., 1956 —.
    Published four times a month on 5 X 8-inch file cards, the data are arranged alphabetically by country and sub-filed under "general," "domestic" or "foreign policy" catagories. Occasionally something is filed by subject, such as "selective service." Since 1968 a compilation of this data into monthly reports called *On Record* has been published. This is an especially useful source for a quick summary or chronology of a recent political event.

Department of State Bulletin. Washington, D.C.: Government
Printing Office.
    Up-to-date information on international relations and the official administration view of American foreign policy is contained herein. Published weekly, it contains messages delivered by the president and speeches delivered by other U. S. officials. It also fills its columns with State Department press releases, terms of new treaties, and analyses of current foreign policy issues.

Dictionaries of Political Science

These specialized subject-matter dictionaries include not only the political meanings of common words and phrases, but also concise definitions, descriptions, and origins of a great many specialized political terms, court cases, organizations, political events, leaders, and so on. The political meanings of such terms as "Hunkerism," "dinosaur," "EPIC plan," "*Scales vs. United States,*" and many other phrases and terms can be found in the following special purpose dictionaries.

> Dunner, Joseph. *Dictionary of Political Science.* New York: Philosophical Library, 1964.
> Elliott, E. *A Dictionary of Politics.* Baltimore, Md.: Penguin Press, 1961.
> Hyamson, A.M. *A Dictionary of International Affairs.* Washington, D.C.: Public Affairs Press, 1946.
> Johnson, Allen. *Dictionary of American Biography.* New York: Charles Scribner's Sons, Inc., 1964.
> McCarthy, E. J. *The Crescent Dictionary of American Politics.* New York: Crowell-Collier-Macmillan, 1962.
> Plano, Jack C., and Milton Greenberg. *The American Political Dictionary.* New York: Holt, Rinehart & Winston, Inc., 1967.
> Smith, Edward C., and Arthur Zurcher. *New Dictionary of American Politics.* New York: Barnes & Noble, Inc., 1968.
> Sperber, Hans, and Travis Trillschuh. *Dictionary of American Political Terms.* New York: McGraw-Hill Book Co., 1962.
> Stephen, Sir Leslie. *Dictionary of National Biography.* New York: Oxford University Press, Inc., 1959-1960.
> Tallman, Marjorie. *Dictionary of American Government.* Ames, Iowa: Littlefield, Adams & Co., 1957.
> White, Wilbur W. *Political Dictionary.* New York: World Publishing Co., 1947.

Directories of Scholars and Professors.

Although the idiosyncracies, political bias and the like concerning professors are common enough campus gossip, the following directories will lead a researcher to the real man behind the lectern. Quite beyond the usual vital statistics, they include academic specialties, governmental and political experience, and a list of the particular professor's publications. *Biographical Directory of The American Political Science Association* (American Political Science Association, 1968) is the key source for political scientists; while the *Directory of American Scholars, a biographical directory,* vol. 1 (New York: Jacques Cattell Press, R. R. Bowker Co., 1963) contains data on the many historians involved in teaching and research for politically related subjects.

Directory of Federal Statistics for Local Areas: A Guide to Sources. Washington, D. C.: Government Printing Office, 1966 —.

This publication is one of the most useful federally-produced aids in tracking data significant at the state and local levels. It is, in a real sense, a source book to federal sources. If a local political or governmental problem is the topic for research, this Bureau of Census directory will give quick access to the most helpful background documents.

Directory of Information Resources in the United States. The National Referral Center for Science and Technology of the Library of Congress, Washington, D. C.: Government Printing Office. Published irregularly.

To obtain material from this source it is necessary to know precisely what it is. This directory contains what librarians term "fugitive material," in that it is material available to the public on request only, and when the supply is exhausted it is unobtainable. This guide will supply a strong list of most federal and federally sponsored agencies (such as the East-West Center of the University of Hawaii), and will describe their activities and the type of data available from each. Most of the material comes in the form of printed government documents and in typewritten and mimeographed reports. The directory is published irregularly. To date only five volumes have been published, two of which are particularly helpful to the political science student: *Social Sciences*, 1965 and *Federal Government*, 1967.

Dissertations

The importance of doctoral dissertations lies in the fact that each one supposedly represents original research in a specialized field. Some do; many do not.

If the dissertation is to be of value, it must offer a thorough examination of a particular problem and a carefully designed plan for dealing with that problem.

Oftentimes the major points of a dissertation may be found in an abstract, so the actual manuscript need not be obtained. Then too, just going down a list of dissertation titles can be of help in choosing a topic and perhaps in suggesting an original approach to it.

The following are the main sources of dissertations:

Dissertation Abstracts. Ann Arbor: University of Michigan. University Microfilm.

As the major source of doctoral dissertations in the United States, this publication offers a brief abstract of each paper, the emphasis lying in the methods and conclusions of the study. Available in both microfilm and full size editions, it is compiled monthly.

Doctoral Dissertations in Political Science in Universities in the United States. Compiled by Walter Beach in the Summer 1968, issue of the *P.S. Newsletter* of the American Political Science Association, Washington, D. C.

Besides including some dissertations not available from University Microfilms, this publication also offers a list of dissertations in progress. Although some are never completed, they can be excellent idea material. Published yearly.

Economic Almanac. New York: New York National Industrial Conference Board, 1940 —.

Although not a comprehensive work, this almanac contains information about business, labor, and government in the more prominent political powers of the world. The statistics of the United States are the most complete. It also contains a general index, a special index on Canada, and a glossary of terms. One can learn, for example, how much the average production worker in Los Angeles earns per hour or how many people will be employed in certain occupations by 1975.

Education Index. New York: H. W. Wilson Co., 1932 —.

This reference, published monthly, except July and August, with compilations, is a subject index to educational periodicals, yearbooks, and bulletins, and the publications of the United States Office of Education from the year 1929. It indexes the answers to such questions as: What is the latest method of educating the mentally handicapped? How much money is being spent by the Federal government on education?

Encyclopedias

Most people instinctively turn to a general reference encyclopedia as their first source of reference, and they are well advised to do so. A good encyclopedia contains not only a great deal of important substantive information, but also useful bibliographies, cross references, and other guides to help in conducting further research. Encyclopedias, however, vary in at least three important ways:

1. *Quality.* Many encyclopedias are authoritative and scholarly, but some are neither. Only those encyclopedias generally accepted as reliable by teachers, librarians, and scholars are listed herein.

2. *Depth.* Some encyclopedias are designed for grade school and high school use, some for popular adult use, and others for scholarly use at the college level. Included here are only those suitable for research at the college level, excluding many excellent works such as the *World Book*, which is designed for elementary, high school, and general adult use.

3. *Scope*. While the term *Encyclopedia* denotes an all-inclusive approach, even encyclopedias specialize. Under the proper title the strong points of each set are indicated.

The Encyclopedia Americana. New York: The Americana Corporation, 1967.

This is the strongest source for all aspects of American life and culture, including, of course, American politics. Articles are written by leading scholars, with especially strong coverage of recent American history. The bibliography is extensive and so authoritative that it is frequently consulted by librarians.

Encyclopaedia Britannica. Chicago: Encyclopaedia Britannica, Inc., 1968.

Although no longer British-oriented, this is without question the single most extensive and detailed general encyclopedia, with some articles in the traditional fields of the humanities, arts, and sciences that have become classics. In scope and depth the major articles are equivalent to specialized books on the subject, but unlike ordinary books a *Britannica* article is assuredly written by an outstanding authority in his field. The assistance of cross references and "sign post" articles to lead to related material in other fields is also given.

Collier's Encyclopedia. New York: Crowell-Collier and Macmillan, Inc., 1969.

This is a strong, clearly written, well-indexed general encyclopedia. It is reliable and often has enough depth for freshman and sophomore assignments, although it is not exhaustive. It is a good first source with excellent bibliographies and indexes.

Compton's Pictured Encyclopedia and Fact-Index. Chicago: Encyclopaedia Britannica, Inc., 1968.

Compton's is a good all-around reference source. Although it does not attempt to provide the depth of the *Britannica* or the *Americana*, it is especially helpful as a first reference source, and the articles are well written and fully keyed to school curricula. There are extensive bibliographies grouped for different educational levels. Each volume has a fact index leading the reader to a large selection of short factual and biographical entries. *Compton's* is a good choice for a first reference.

Encyclopedia International. New York: The Grolier Club, 1968.

It is difficult to publish a new encyclopedia that can compete in scope and quality with the established sets, but the *Encyclopedia International* is doing just that. It is a general encyclopedia similar to *Compton's* and *Collier's*. It is especially readable, with unusual headings and subheadings that heighten reader interest; it also includes such helpful and practical information as lists of colleges, study aids, and career guides.

Encyclopedia of the Social Sciences. E. R. A. Seligman, ed. New York: Crowell-Collier and Macmillan Inc., 1930-1935.

Hundreds of international scholars prepared this comprehensive survey of the fields of social science in the early 1930's. They have produced a work that is considered to be the most important in this field. Somewhat out-of-date today, it should be used with the newer *International Encyclopedia of Social Sciences*, though the editors of the newer work did not intend to supersede the older volumes. This set contains many classic articles by leading social scientists, articles that helped to define an entire field of study. The seventeen volumes include a 349-page introduction in two parts: a discussion of the meaning of the social sciences and an outline of their chronological development, and a nation-by-nation survey of the disciplines involved in the social sciences. The main portion of the work deals with the important concepts in political sciences, economics, law, anthropology, sociology, penology, and social work. About a quarter of the work is composed of biographical sketches. All entries are alphabetically arranged with cross references and a subject index.

An Encyclopedia of World History. William L. Langer, ed. Boston: Houghton Mifflin Co., 1968.

In no other volume can one locate the essential facts of world history so quickly. Using an expanded outline form with important names and dates in boldface type, this single volume covers the recorded history of the world. Extensively indexed, it allows one to spend a minimum of effort in finding such data as the chronology of the short Soviet-Finno war of 1939-1940, or the Moslem conquest of Spain in 711-1031.

The Encyclopedia of U.S. Government Benefits. R.A. Grisham, Jr., ed., in consultation with P.D. McConaughy. Union City, N.J.: Wm. H. Wise & Co., Inc., 1965.

This reference book lists, describes, and discusses all services and benefits provided by the United States government. It provides answers to the complex question of the citizen's relationship to big government. This is the first book to catalog and detail eligibility for all government services. It is also unique in alphabetizing primarily by benefit classification rather than by agency, department, or initiating legislative act. It is both a practical reference and a useful index to the scope and depth of federal programs.

Essay and General Literature Index. New York: H. W. Wilson, Co., 1934.

This index, published semiannually with accumulations, specifically catalogs books rather than periodicals, which is helpful because often essays and articles appear in books of collected works without there being a specific reference to them in the title. This index could help locate, for example, an article on "Woodrow Wilson and Southern Congressmen" which appeared in a book edited by Sidney Fine, titled *Recent America* (New York: Crowell-Collier and Macmillan, Inc., 1962).

Everyman's United Nations. New York: United Nations Department of Public Information, 1964.

This is the primary source for the structure, functions, and work of the United Nations and its related agencies. This frequently revised handbook is broken into four parts: Part I discusses the organization of the United Nations; Part II is concerned with political, social, economic, and security questions; Part III deals with specialized agencies, such as the Food and Agriculture Organization (FAO), the United Nations Educational, Scientific, and Cultural Organization (UNESCO), and many others; Part IV gives an index, the chronology, and a list of the United Nations Information Centers.

Facts about the Presidents. New York: H.W. Wilson Co., 1968.

This volume contains much information about the presidents of the United States in a quick, easy-to-use form. It even compares the presidents in such areas as the size of their parents and families, their own physical appearances, last words, etc.

Facts on File: World News Digest. New York: Facts on File, 1940 —.

This publication records the events of each week in an unbiased and concise style. Each news item is filed and reported under a specific heading such as world affairs, national affairs, sports, and the like. Each also includes a reference to any previous article on the same topic. However, sources are not listed. Four five-year indexes have been issued so far for the years 1946-1950, 1951-1955, 1956-1961, and 1962-1967.

Familiar Quotations. John Bartlett, ed. Boston: Little, Brown and Co., 1955.

This is a useful collection of thousands of quotations that have become part of the English language. Bartlett lists each quotation under its author and reprints it within the context of the poem, passage, or article in which it originally appeared. The authors are listed chronologically, and there is a topical index referring to page and author. For instance, the source of the line, "What this country needs is a good five-cent cigar," can be found under *cigar* in the line index. (The source of this quotation, incidentally, is Thomas R. Marshall, the vice-president under Woodrow Wilson.)

Federal Career Directory: A Guide for College Students. United States Civil Service Commission. Washington, D.C.: Government Printing Office, 1956—.

This is one of a dozen or so guides to federal employment. The commission's regional offices also publish separate local guides.

Federal Register. Washington, D.C.: Government Printing Office, 1936—.

Published five times a week, the *Federal Register* includes presidential executive orders, proclamations, reorganization plans, and rules and regulations issued by executive departments and agencies. It is accurate and complete and is the best source on executive affairs.

Foreign Affairs Bibliography. New York: Council on Foreign Affairs. 1962.

This is actually a ready-made bibliography on even the most specialized foreign policy topics of the United States and other nations. Organized nation-by-nation as well as by topic, it contains such subheadings as Liberalism, Conservatism, colonial problems, labor movements, human rights, the Cold War, and brief annotations that include books, research series and documents.

Foreign Relations of the United States: Diplomatic Papers. Washington, D. C.: Government Printing Office, 1852 —.

This is a Department of State series that offers the most complete State Department records of the past. Published approximately every twenty years, a series set lists a year-by-year selection of public documents, diplomatic correspondence, messages between the U. S. and other governments, and departmental memorandums.

Great Books of the Western World and The Great Ideas. a Syntopticon. Mortimer J. Adler, ed. Chicago: Encyclopedia Britannica, Inc. 1961.

The two-volume *Syntopticon* contains an analytic essay for each of the 102 "great ideas." These essays break down and analyze each idea, illustrating in the process the intellectual handles of each. Under "law," for instance, is a clear and succinct approach to the idea of law — divine and natural law, and the relationship of law and the individual. The remaining fifty-four volumes contain the works of the great thinkers and writers of Western civilization. To these fifty-four volumes the essays of the *Syntopticon* are keyed, permitting one to trace the development of an idea through history or to compare the views of two or more giants of history. Each of the 102 essays is cross-indexed, providing innumerable approaches to a single subject.

Government Publications and Their Use. 2nd rev. ed. Laurence F. Schmeckebier and Roy B. Eastin. Washington, D. C.: The Brookings Institution, 1969.

This publication describes the basic guides to government publications; indicates the uses and limitations of available indexes, catalogs, and bibliographies; explains the systems of numbering; calls attention to outstanding compilations or series; and directs the student in the various ways of obtaining the publications. This second edition reflects the many changes and the growth in the number of government publications over the last ten years. Referring to the first edition, *Library Journal* remarked: "Nowhere but in Schmeckebier is there such a clear exposition of the quirks involved in the issuing of government documents, and the best ways to work with indexes and keys to this primary research material."

Guide to Reference Books. 8th ed. Constance M. Winchell, ed. Chicago: American Library Association, 1967.

The most comprehensive of all guides of this type, the *Guide to Reference Books* was first published in 1902 and through eight editions has kept conspicuously up-to-date. The last edition divides 7,500 titles into five catagories: general reference works; humanities; social sciences; history and area studies; and the pure and applied sciences. Political science, of course, is included in the social sciences section.

Guide to Reference Material in Political Science. Lubomyr R. Wynan. Rochester, New York: Libraries Unlimited, Inc.

This reference consists of two volumes of a conventionally organized and extensively annotated guide to bibliographies. Generally it provides an acceptable basic bibliography for the basic fields of political science.

Guides to Study

The choice of a graduate or undergraduate program is one of the most important decisions a student must make. Unfortunately, it is quite difficult to obtain a comprehensive view of the schools available. The authors, therefore, have included the following guides to provide a broad and detailed comparison of important graduate and undergraduate programs in political science.

The Annual Guide to Graduate Study. Karen C. Hegener. Princeton, N. J.: Peterson's Guides Incorporated.

Such basic facts as the size of library facilities, financial aid, faculty research and student life are outlined field by field, area by area.

Undergraduate Study Abroad. Stephen A. Freeman. New York: Institute of International Education, 1966.

This comprehensive guide presents all the important dates concerning the special overseas program offered by a number of universities. The programs range from summer to full-year schedules, some of which require a foreign language, others which do not.

The World of Learning. Rochester Kent. Europe Publications, London: 1947.

Basic descriptions and a list of responsible individuals in a worldwide directory of colleges, universities, research institutes, museums, libraries, and archives are included in *The World of Learning.*

Guide to the Diplomatic History of the United States. Samuel Flagg Bemis and Grace Gardner Griffin, ed. Washington, D. C.: Government Printing Office, 1935. Reprinted by Peter Smith, 1951.

This guide is the best source extant for facts on American diplomatic history up to 1935. Part I guides one chronologically toward books, journals, chapters of books, manuscript collections and maps. Part II leads one to the best government sources, explaining how to locate them en route.

Guide to the Study of International Relations. J. K. Zawodny. San Francisco: Chandler Publishing Co., 1966.

This guide is a paperback volume designed to aid the student and researcher find the widely scattered and often complex materials tied to the study of international relations — government documents, national archives, UN publications, and up-to-date, empirically validated findings in the behavioral sciences. It holds more than 500 cross-indexed entries classified under subject headings which, except for the journals, have been annotated and can guide the student efficiently through several million titles to the specific ones he desires.

A Guide to the Use of United Nations Documents (Including Reference to the Specialized Agencies and Special UN Bodies). Brenda Brimmer. Doobs Ferry, N.Y.: Oceana Publications, Inc., 1962 —.

Another guide-type volume, this publication supplies the researcher with an exhaustive description of the documents classification system, a list of the many UN publications, and various approaches to research projects in general.

Historical Atlas. William Robert Shepherd. New York: Barnes & Noble, Inc., 1964.

This is a superb one-volume atlas covering the world from about 1945 B.C. to the present. Each map is arranged chronologically (there is no accompanying text). The volume contains an exhaustive index of place names, including classical and medieval Latin place names, many of which do not appear on the maps. These are cross-referenced to the modern forms of the names.

Historical Statistics of the United States, Colonial Times to 1957. Washington, D.C.: Government Printing Office, 1960.

This is a supplement to the *Statistical Abstract of the United States*, which contains more than 8,000 statistical studies grouped mostly into yearly periods. It covers economic and social development from 1610 to 1957 and includes definitions of terms and descriptive text. Source notes provide a guide for students who wish to read the original published sources for further reference and data. It contains a complete subject index alphabetically arranged. The work also includes about 300 series that are complements to or substitutes for any series discontinued since 1956.

Historical Statistics of the United States, Colonial Times to 1957: Continuation to 1962 and Revisions. U. S. Bureau of Census. Washington, D. C.: Government Printing Office, 1965.

This volume includes the same general type of statistics as in the basic statistical abstract, but the data is rearranged into comparative historical periods.

How to Locate Educational Information and Data. Carter Alexander and Arbid Burke, Jr. New York: Teachers College Press, 1958.

Although it is directed toward the education major, other students may benefit from this handbook's basic instruction in the use of the library. It describes reference sources, card catalogs, periodical indexes, bibliographies, and government documents, enabling the student to locate the information that he requires.

Index to Legal Periodicals. New York: H. W. Wilson Co., 1909 —.

Law journals interpret the law; they also are an excellent source of public policy articles such as the regulation of business. This, the best of law journals, contains roughly 300 journals and is published monthly with annual cumulations.

International Bibliography of Political Science. The International Committee for Social Science Documentation. Chicago: Aldine Publishing Co., 1954 —.

These annual volumes contain a select worldwide list of the most important books and articles in social science areas. The topics are often highly specialized.

International Bibliography of Political Science. Paris: UNESCO, 1954—.

This reference has been published annually since 1952 by the International Committee for Social Sciences Documentation under the auspices of the International Political Science Association. As the title suggests, it includes an international selection of the most important publications of the discipline.

International Political Science Abstracts. Oxford: Basil Blackwell, 1951 —.

Prepared (quarterly) by the International Political Science Association and the International Studies Conference, with the support of the Coordination Committee on Documentation in the Social Sciences, each volume contains about 350 abstracts, including 150 abstracted journals. In the first volume, a very broad subject group is arranged with an author and subject index. Subsequently, the arrangement is alphabetical by author, with cumulated subject and author indexes in the fourth issue of each year. Abstracts of articles in English are in English; those articles in other languages are translated into French only.

International Who's Who. London: G. Allen, 1935 —.

Published annually since 1935, this reference contains from 8,000 to 13,000 short biographical sketches of prominent figures of the world. Before 1935 it formed a part of the looseleaf service called "Europa." The *International Who's Who* provides brief but reliable information on the subjects, giving name, title, dates, nationality, education, profession, career, works, and address.

International Yearbook and Statesmen's Who's Who. London: Burke's Peerage, 1953 —.

This volume combines data on political and economic conditions of the world with an international biographical directory of about 10,000 individuals of world renown: statesmen, diplomats, military leaders, clergy, industrialists, and so forth. The information on various nations, arranged alphabetically, is similar to that in the *Statesman's Yearbook* but with more statistical details.

Inter-University Consortium for Political Research. Ann Arbor, Michigan: The University of Michigan Press.

This is the most prestigious of the academic data sources. It keeps abreast of most academic surveys, research projects, and similar data as produced by the academic community. The poll results go beyond simple preference questions, such as "Who are you going to vote for?", and probes motivation, attitudes and interelationships, such as "What made you switch from Bobby Kennedy to George Wallace?" Data is available at a nominal fee.

Issues before the General Assemblies of the United Nations: 1946-1965. New York: Arno Press, Inc., 1970.

This is a specially compiled selection of excerpts from the major speeches and issues on the General Assembly agenda since its first session in 1946. Also compiled for this edition is a cumulative index which allows the student to find in one source basic information concerning relevant problems facing the United Nations — a good "first stop" for a term paper.

Keesing's Contemporary Archives: Weekly Diary of World Events. W. Rosenberger and H. C. Tobin, ed. London: Keesing's Publications Ltd, 1931 —.

These volumes are mainly a wrapup of news reports for the week, but they also include recent speeches and government documents, prominent obituaries, etc. This service covers world events but is strongest for the United Kingdom and Europe. It is indexed cumulatively into capsules of two weeks, three months, a year and two years.

Masterpieces of World Philosophy in Summary Form. Frank N. Magill, ed. New York: Harper & Row, Publishers, 1963.

Some academicians feel that students of philosophy or political theory must gain their understanding from the original works of the philosophers themselves with little or no outside assistance. There is room for disagreement. While it is always beneficial to read the original, most students can help sharpen their understanding by outside direction. A glance at one of the summaries offered is likely to raise the student's level of comprehension. Also, there are times when it is neither wise nor possible to read an entire work, in which case this reference can save the day.

Metropolitan Area Annual. J. F. Zimmerman, ed. Albany, N. Y.: State University at Albany, Graduate School of Public Affairs, 1967 —.

Published annually, this work contains the latest developments in municipal government, various city statistics, directories of municipal officials, directories of state agencies at the local affairs level, and metropolitan area planning commissions. The articles summarize municipal developments in a given year. For example, if one wished to know the Safe Streets Act or some other federal program on municipalities, this annual would provide a quick summary.

Municipal Yearbook. Chicago: International City Managers' Association, 1934—.

This annual reference is certainly the best source in its field. It is an authoritative résumé of activities and statistical data of American cities, with emphasis on individual city programs. Attention is devoted to developments in urban counties and metropolitan areas. One can also find in it thorough bibliographies and comprehensive directories of officials.

National Journal. Cliff Sessions, ed. Washington, D. C.: Center for Political Research, 1970 —.

This journal was founded by a group of editors and reporters who left *Congressional Quarterly* because they felt it did not pay enough attention to bureaucratic decision-making. The *Journal* is published weekly and designed as a monitor of all government actions. It does more than record government action; it analyzes all the details surrounding such actions, focusing mainly on the relationships between the various power-wielding agencies that cram the nation's capital. The interests involved in any issue are plainly identified — this, in itself, cuts away much of the arcane for the student. It also contains in-depth reports on federal programs, biographical information on government officials, and analyses of congressional districts.

National Party Platforms 1840-1960. Kirk Porter and Donald Johnson. Urbana: University of Illinois Press. With supplements.

Even though a political party platform is not often followed after elections, it must be considered as an indicator of the goals and internal dissentions of the party. Included are the platforms of many minor parties, as well as the two major parties. In 1960, for example, this work included the platforms of Democratic, Republican, Prohibition Socialist, Socialist, Labor, and Socialist Worker parties.

New International Yearbook. New York: Funk & Wagnalls, 1932 —.

This reference work charts the events and progress of the year, classifying each under categories such as politics, foreign affairs, labor, sports, and so on. It is indexed and includes photographs, charts, and detailed statistics.

New York Times Index. New York: The New York Times, 1913 —.

This index is the major reference source for an accurate chronological list of important events. Published semimonthly with annual cumulations since 1930, this publication presents an extensive and detailed look at the world news as reported by the *New York Times.* It cites the date, page, and column with many cross references, and serves as a reference for material in other newspapers as well. One of the features students find most attractive is the brief synopsis under each entry, which frequently makes reference to the newspaper itself unnecessary. An earlier index covering the years 1851-1858 and 1860-1905 is available on microfilm.

Opinion Polls

California Poll. San Francisco: Survey Research Services, Inc.

The California electorate is one of the most significant in the nation as a harbinger of future trends. This poll is concentrated within the State of California. It polls Californians on the hottest issue at the time and publishes results between thirty-five to forty-five times a year. A year's subscription costs $25.

Gallup Opinion Index. Princeton, N. J.: Gallup International, 1965 —.

Although most Americans are familiar with the Gallup opinion polls published regularly in many newspapers, these polls are often neglected by undergraduate researchers because of the difficulty of locating a particular poll in an unindexed newspaper. This monthly publication offers an answer to this problem through the publication of thirteen to fifteen monthly surveys covering a wide range of subjects, from Vietnam to the "Most Admired Woman."

Minnesota Poll. Otto A. Silha, ed. Minneapolis: The Minneapolis Star and Tribune Co., 1964 —.

This poll is published with the Sunday editions of the *Minneapolis Tribune* with a twenty-year summary published in 1964 under the title, *Twenty Years of Minnesota Opinion, 1944-1964: Minneapolis Tribunes' Minnesota Poll.*

Roper Public Opinion Poll. Williamstown, Mass.: Williams College.

The most exhaustive file of poll data in existence, this source concentrates on all academic and professional poll and survey groups from around the world. The surveys and studies are available to students on cards or tapes at quite reasonable rates.

Political Handbook and Atlas of The World. Walter Mallory, ed. New York: Council on Foreign Relations, 1927 —.

This annual paperback contains an alphabetical listing of the factual background (heavily political) of all the independent nations of the world and is supplemented with a section of detailed maps. It includes such data as a nation's political structure, its major news media, its land area, its population, and an outline of its political history.

Poole's Index to Periodical Literature, rev. ed. Boston: Houghton Mifflin Co., 1891.

Although not as comprehensive as the *Reader's Guide to Periodical Literature*, this is still the best index of nineteenth-century periodicals. It includes poems and stories and covers approximately the years 1800-1906. It can be used to research such a subject as the political attitudes expressed in American periodicals of that time.

Popular Names of U. S. Government Reports. Donald Wisdom and William P. Kilroy. Washington, D. C.: Library of Congress, 1966.

For reasons in strict keeping with governmental practices, while many significant reports are popularly known by the name of one of the responsible officials, their name is seldom part of the official title. This guide leads you to the exact citation when all you have to work on is something such as "The Kerner Report."

Public Affairs Information Service Index. New York: Public Affairs Information Service, Inc., 1915 —.

This index, with annual cumulations, unifies a wide variety of sources concerned with public affairs. Besides periodicals it lists books, pamphlets, and government documents. The subjects include economics, social conditions, politics, and international relations. Its bibliography is adequate for identification, and most articles include brief explanatory items.

Random House Guide to Graduate Study in the Arts & Sciences. E. R. Wasserman and E. E. Switzer. New York: Random House, Inc., 1967.

This guide summarizes graduate programs in all fields and contains helpful chapters on the nature of graduate study, how to apply to a graduate school, and test questions from the Graduate Record Examination.

Readers' Guide to Periodical Literature. New York: H. W. Wilson Co., 1901 —.

This is the major periodical reference book, a book which lists author and subject in separate indexes referring to the most popular, non-technical periodicals in the English language.

Reader's Guide to the Social Sciences. Bert F. Hoselitz, ed. Glencoe, Illinois: The Free Press, 1959 —.

This is broken down into sections of history, geography, sociology, anthropology, psychology, economics and political science. The last chapter is written by Heinz Eulau, who presents a splendid introduction to the more important studies in political science.

Reference Books in the Social Sciences and Humanities. Rolland E. Stevens. Champaign, Illinois: Illinois Union Bookstore, 1968—.

The second edition of this volume was published in 1968. It offers an annotated list of reference materials on such topics as political science, law, and public administration.

Robert's Rules of Order. Glenview, Ill.: Scott, Foresman and Co., 1951.

Written by Henry M. Robert in 1876, this book perscribes the way to organize and conduct meetings, lists the duties of officers, and describes the proper function of motions and amendments. Its style is clear and easy to follow, and it is comprehensive enough to answer most questions on proper meeting procedures.

Select Bibliography: Asia, Africa, Eastern Europe, Latin America. New York: American University, 1960.

Since 1960 the so-called developing countries of the world have become a recurring theme of academic attention. Today they are the center of international politics and, hence, a prime target of undergraduate study and theses. Here will be found current books and academic journal articles listed by geographic or subject area of interest. It is unusual among bibliographies in that it makes a systematic qualitative distinction between first choice, labeled *A*, and second choice, labeled *B*.

Selected United States Government Publications. Washington, D.C.: Government Printing Office.

The government prints and mails out a biweekly list of the thousands of pamphlets, books, and periodicals published by the Government Printing Office. Writer-researchers are sent into the field by the government to initiate exhaustive research into topics as varied as the ones following. One may place one's name on the free mailing list by sending name and address to: Superintendent of Documents, United States Government Printing Office, Washington, D. C. The order form is attached to the lists and includes topics such as black-white differences in geographic mobility, health information (menopause, varicose veins, high blood pressure, and so on), the Great Seal of the United States, heart disease in adults, United States from 1960 to 1971, boating regulations in the national park system, employment and earnings statistics for states and areas, and case studies of displaced workers. Prices vary, but most pamphlets and books cost less than comparable volumes privately printed.

Social Sciences and Humanities Index. New York: H. W. Wilson Co., 1916 —.

This index, which has quarterly compilations, provides the best source for developing an academic or theoretical focus for a term paper. For example, in referring to general headings such as "inteest groups" one will find scholarly articles outlining the pros and cons of the various political science approaches to the study of interest groups, articles that will provide a useful frame of reference for the study of a particular group. In June, 1965 the name of this reference was changed from *International Index* in order to indicate more accurately the scope of its coverage.

Sources of Information in the Social Sciences: A Guide to the Literature. Carl M. White et al. Totowa, N. J.: The Bedminster Press, 1964.

Besides general reference works, this source offers a separate treatment to history, economics and business administration, sociology, anthropology, psychology, education, and political science. Each chapter is complete with introduction, important studies, bibliographies, and data sources. The volume is geared for the interdisciplinary and behavioral approach to the social sciences.

Statesman's Year Book: Statistical and Historical Annual of the States of the World. M. Epstien, ed. Ltd. London, Melbourne and Toronto: The Macmillan Co.; New York: St. Martin's Press, 1864 —.

A general yearbook of more than general value, this book offers a yearly update of economic, political and social statistics and information on international organizations, and on every country functioning during the preceding year. The data include each nation's constitution, political and governmental structure, financial basis, gross national product, court system, etc.

Statistical Abstract for Latin America. Berkeley, Calif.: University of California Press, 1956 —.

This annually-issued volume presents current statistical data on all Latin American nations and their dependencies. Information is offered on area, population, social organization, economic characteristics, finances, foreign trade, and other special topics. Notes and source information accompany its tables; it contains an adequate bibliography.

Statistical Abstract of the United States. Washington, D. C.: Government Printing Office 1879 —.

Published annually, this work is a recognized, reliable summary of statistics on the social, political, and economic organization of the United States. It also serves as a guide to other statistical publications and sources through the introductory text to each section, the source notes for each table, and the bibliography of sources. Here one can find information of primarily national concern. Also included are many tables for regions and individual states and statistics for the commonwealth of Puerto Rico and other outlying areas of the United States.

Additional information for cities, counties, metropolitan areas, congressional districts, and other small units is available in supplements to the abstract (such as *County and City Data Book; Congressional District Data Book; Historical Statistics of the U.S., Colonial Times to 1957; and Historical Statistics of the U.S., Colonial Times to 1957, Continuation to 1962 and Revisions*). The *Statistical Abstract* is the most reliable source for such data as births; deaths; marriages and divorces; number of physicians, dentists and nurses; immigration and naturalization; law enforcement, courts, and prisons; geography and climate; public lands and parks; recreation and travel; elections; and incomes.

Subject Guide to Major Government Publications. Ellen Jackson. Chicago: American Library Association, 1968.

Few researchers, on starting their inquiry, can identify the important government publications revelant to their topic. This publication gives an annotated bibliography of key government documents cn general topics, such as "nuclear rearmament," as well as suggested cross references.

Taylor's Encyclopedia of Government Officials (Federal and State). John Clements, ed. Dallas, Texas: Political Research, Inc., 1970—.

This encyclopedia is an accurate and continually updated work containing complete information on every major federal and state governmental body in the United States. From the president to the state party chairmen, it includes names, photographs, and frequently even home addresses. Changes due to new appointments, elections, redistricting, and other events are available to subscribers, and the entire book is reprinted every two years to include updated material. It can save the student hours of research.

Treaties in Force. Washington, D.C.: Government Printing Office, 1929, printed irregularly until 1958, annually thereafter.

Each year the Government Printing Office publishes a list of treaties and other international agreements to which the United States has become a party. Bilateral treaties are arranged by nation; multilateral treaties, by subject. Because of its narrow scope, this reference is both simple to use and thorough in its treatment.

*United Nations Documents Index (*also *The Annual Cumulative Index).* Dag Hammarskjold Library, New York, N. Y.: Documents Index Unit, United Nations Publications, published monthly, 1950 —.

The UN documentation system is shockingly cryptographic, and would be impossible to penetrate without the key. A general description of the documents is to be found in *A Guide to the Use of United Nations Documents* (see p. 86). But the index must be used if one is to keep abreast or locate specific documents.

United Nations Statistical Yearbook. New York: United Nations Statistical Office, 1949 —.

This is a continuation of the *Statistical Yearbook of the League of Nations, 1927-1945.* The upheaval of World War II caused the gap between 1945 and 1949. Its tables cover world population, manpower, agriculture, production, mining construction, consumption, transportation, external trade, wages, prices, national income, finance, social statistics, education, and culture. A ten-to-twenty-year period is generally given for each series. Its sources are cited, it contains subject and nation indexes, and its text is written in French and English. Current data for many tables are published regularly by the United Nations Statistical Office *Monthly Bulletin of Statistics* (which has been in existence since 1947).

United Nations World Economic Survey. New York: United Nations Statistical Office, 1945 —.

Yearly charts interpret the economy trends of the world in this survey. This book spawns a supplement of detailed studies of entire continental regions.

United Nations World Survey of Education. New York: United Nations Statistical Office, 1955.

This guide has been published four times, but has not, to date, followed a formal publishing schedule. The four volumes extant deal with educational organizations and statistics (1955); primary education (1958); secondary education (1961); and higher education (1966).

United Nations Yearbook of National Accounts Statistics. New York: United Nations Statistical Office, 1954 —.

This reference concerns itself with the gross national product (GNP) of each nation and generally includes a rather complete financial picture (government spending and income, consumer consumption, etc.).

United States Code & United States Statutes At Large. Washington, D.C.: Government Printing Office, 1875 —.

The *United States Code* is published every six years, with an annual supplement. This is the source to consult for a paper on any legislation that has been passed by Congress. It is the source of up-to-date public laws covering every topic. Another source for public laws is *United States Statutes At Large,* a study that breaks down the public laws into two parts: first, all public laws that were passed during a particular year; and second, all private bills passed. Laws in both books are classified under fifty titles, such as public lands, education, defense, Congress and banks. (As to how to find U.S. Statutes and Code citations turn to page 107).

There are also commercially published editions of this work known as *United States Code Annotated* (St. Paul, Minn.: West Publishing Company, 1927 —) and *Federal Code Annotated* (New York & Indianapolis, Ind.: Bobbs-Merrill Company, 1937 —). These annotated editions include notes on judicial interpretations of the law as well as the law itself. If available, they are more useful than the *United States Code.*

If one is interested in state rather than federal laws the proper source would be individual state codes.

United States Government Organization Manual. Washington, D.C.: Government Printing Office, 1935 —.

This annually published study is the prime source for the current organization and functions of each of the departments and agencies that make up the executive branch. It is the official organization handbook of the federal government and contains sections describing the agencies of the legislative, judicial, and executive branches. It also presents brief descriptions of quasi-official agencies and of selected international organizations. This manual may also serve as a source of ideas for term papers.

United States in World Affairs. The Council on Foreign Relations. New York: Harper & Row Publishers, 1967 —.

Published yearly, this book is a series of interpretive essays that try to explain American foreign policy. A detailed chronology in the appendix makes this series most useful as an integrator of events. For example, the contents for 1966 list: "What Price a Free Vietnam"; "Origins of the Problem's Two Views"; "End of the Pause"; "Honolulu and After"; "The Debate Continues and So Does the War."

United States Reports. Washington, D.C.: Government Printing Office, 1790 —.

This is a compilation of each decision rendered by the United States Supreme Court. Most decisions include majority, dissenting, and concurring opinions. These opinions contain the sweep of facts, attitudes, and legal concepts relating to the important issues which come before the Supreme Court.

United States Treaties and Other International Agreements. Washington, D.C.: Government Printing Office.

This is an annual publication listing (as the title claims) all treaties and agreements to which the United States has become a party during a given year.

Universal Reference System. New Jersey: Princeton Research Co., 1969.

This source consists of a ten-volume set of references costing a library over $1,000, but it can be a worthwhile investment. It will take approximately twenty minutes to master Professor Alfred de Grazia's unique computerized index system; once done, specialized high-quality bibliographies are available. Each of the volumes covers a major area of political science, such as international affairs, legislative decision-making, administrative management, law, jurisprudence and judicial process. Each lists and summarizes thousands of books, articles, papers, and documents selected by the leading political scholars of our day.

Vital Speeches of the Day. New York: City News Publishing Co., 1934—.

This monthly journal prints verbatim important speeches (usually in full) of recognized leaders of public opinion in America. Generally, it covers both sides of public questions, thereby offering the significant thought of leading minds on current national problems.

The journal explains that its purpose is to offer students "the finest textbook material . . . from those who have attained leadership in the fields of politics, economics, education, sociology, government, criminology, finance, business, taxation, health, law, labor. . . ."

Weekly Compilation of Presidential Documents. Washington, D.C.: Government Printing Office, 1965 —.

Published every Monday under the auspices of the Office of the Federal Register, National Archives and Records Service, and General Services Administration, this source contains the presidential materials released by the White House up to 5 P.M. the preceding Friday. It includes the president's addresses, remarks, announcements, appointments and nominations, executive orders, memoranda, meetings with foreign leaders, and proclamations, as well as reports to the president.

Who's Who in America: A Biographical Dictionary of Notable Living Men and Women. Chicago: A.N. Marquis Co., 1899 —.

One political scientist has described this book as "An authoritative dictionary of contemporary biography, including the best known men and women in all lines of useful and reputable achievement — names much in the public eye, not names locally but generally." The biographies fall into two groups: those selected because of their special prominence or distinction in certain fields and those included arbitrarily due to their official position or public standing. Included are not only American citizens, but all persons of any nationality likely to be of interest to Americans. It is supplemented by: *Who Was Who in America*, for all persons deleted due to death; *The Monthly Supplement*, December 1939 to 1956; the *Supplement to Who's Who*, issued quarterly since 1957; the *Ten-Year Cumulative Index, 1939-1949*; and the *Cumulative Index for 1951-1955*. The publication major is revised and reissued biennially with monthly supplements.

Who's Who in American Politics. Paul A. Theis and Edmund L. Henshaw, Jr., ed. New York: R.R. Bowker Co., 1968.

This work, first published to cover the 1967-68 period, is a biographical directory of 12,500 political leaders in the United States. It is a thorough and authoritative publication bearing the credentials of both major political parties. The biographical material was gathered mostly by questionaires, but the editors note in the introduction: "In some cases when we felt the prominence of a biographee warranted his inclusion even though his questionaire was not returned, biographical data was gathered from various sources, and a proof copy was prepared which the biographee was asked to verify before it was included in the directory."

World Almanac and Book of Facts. New York: Newspaper Enterprise Association, 1868 —.

Published yearly, first by the *New York World-Telegram and Sun*, the *World Almanac* supplies a wealth of information in every area likely to be investigated by undergraduate students. A random sample of the broad spectrum of the work includes the latest sports records; Nobel Prize recipients; listings of college and universities; heads of states; brief descriptions of foreign countries; a list of United States art galleries; biographies of presidents and their wives, cabinet members, Supreme Court judges, and ambassadors; and an explanation of how to make out a will properly.

In the same category as the *World Almanac* and furnishing basically the same information are: *Information Please Almanac* (New York: Simon & Schuster, Inc.); and *Reader's Digest Almanac*, edited by *Reader's Digest* editors (New York: Funk & Wagnalls).

Worldmark Encyclopedia of Nations. New York: Harper & Row, Publishers, 1963.

This three-volume work presents the geographic, social, historical, and political facts concerning the nations of the world in an easy-to-use form. There are large standard subheadings, so one can, for instance, compare the "transportation system" in Nigeria and Morocco quickly and easily. The third volume offers the same type of detailed factual information for the United Nations and its subsidiary organizations.

Yearbook of International Organizations. Eyvind S. Tew, ed. Brussels, Belgium: Union of International Associations.

Of the more than 2,000 international organizations listed herein, less than 50 are affiliated with the United Nations — a fact that gives many a young scholar pause. Of course, those not carrying UN credentials do not often make the front pages, but in their particular area, they are quite influential; without a guide of this type, they would undoubtedly elude most students. Those not carrying UN credentials include a range from the highly political International Peace Association to the relatively esoteric International Association of Art Critics. Each entry covers the general history and a description of the organization and — more important — a direction to sources of further information.

Yearbook of the United Nations. New York: United Nations Department of Public Information, 1947 —.

These annual editions constitute a year-by-year record of the activities of the United Nations. Each edition is designed to present within a single, fully indexed volume a compact authoritative account of the deliberations and actions of the United Nations, as well as the activities of the intergovernmental agencies related to it.

PART III

POLITICAL SCIENTISTS: A RANKING

Every field has its great names, with which a serious student of the field should be familiar. The names listed are those of leaders in the study of political science. The list was based on a 1962-survey of 832 political scientists by Albert Somit and Joseph Tanenhaus for their book *American Political Science* (New York: Atherton Press, Inc., 1964).

Rank (pre-1945)

1	Charles E. Merriam
2	Harold D. Lasswell
3	Leonard D. White
4	Charles A. Beard
5	Edward S. Corwin
6	Arthur F. Bentley
7	Woodrow Wilson
8	Pendleton Herring
9	Quincy Wright
10	Frederic A. Ogg
11	Frank J. Goodnow
12.5	Harold J. Laski
12.5	Arthur H. Holcombe
14.5	Francis W. Coker

Rank (post-1945)

1	V. O. Key, Jr.
2	David B. Truman
3	Hans J. Morgenthau
4	Robert A. Dahl
5	Harold D. Lasswell
6	Herbert A. Simon
7.5	Gabriel A. Almond
7.5	David Easton
9	Leo Strauss
10	Carl J. Friedrich
11	Charles S. Hyneman
12	E. E. Schattschneider
13.5	Peter H. Odegard
13.5	Richard C. Snyder

14.5 Carl J. Friedrich
16   George H. Sabine
17.5 Harold F. Gosnell
17.5 E. E. Schattschneider

15   Leonard D. White
17   James M. Burns
17   Karl W. Deutsch
17   Heinz Eulau
17   Dwight Waldo

POLITICAL SCIENCE DEPARTMENTS: A RANKING

The student who is considering graduate school in political science may be guided by the following list from a survey published in Albert Somit and Joseph Tanenhaus, *American Political Science* (New York: Atherton Press, Inc., 1964).

1   Harvard University
2   Yale University
3   University of California at Berkeley
4   University of Chicago
5   Princeton University
6   Columbia University
7   University of Michigan
8.5   University of Wisconsin
8.5   Stanford University
10.5 University of California at Los Angeles
10.5 Cornell University
12   Johns Hopkins University
13   Northwestern University
14   Indiana University
15   University of Illinois
16   University of Minnesota

17   University of Nort Carolina
18.5 Duke University
18.5 Syracuse University
20   University of Pennsylvania
21   Vanderbilt University
22   New York University
23   Michigan State University
24.5 University of Iowa
24.5 Ohio State University
26   University of Washington
27.5 Georgetown University
27.5 University of Texas
29   American University
30   Notre Dame
31   George Washington University
32   Fordham University
33   Catholic University of America

The American Council on Education has also issued a report on the quality of graduate programs at major universities in the United States. The study was made public on January 3, 1971 and was based on a survey of more than 6,000 scholars who rated faculties and programs in 36 fields of study at 130 graduate schools. It would be interesting to compare these findings of the political science departments with those of Somit and Tanenhaus.

1   Yale University
2   Harvard University

4.5 University of Chicago
4.5 Mass. Institute of Technology

4.5	University of Michigan	14	Indiana University
4.5	Stanford University	14	Northwestern University
8	University of North Carolina	14	University of California at Los Angeles
8	Princeton University		
8	University of Wisconsin	16.5	University of Iowa
10	University of California at Berkeley	18.5	Cornell University
11.5	University of Minnesota	18.5	University of Washington at St. Louis
11.5	University of Rochester		

TOP TEN JOURNALS IN THE AREA OF POLITICAL SCIENCE

As rated by Albert Somit and Joseph Tanenhaus, *American Political Science* (New York: Atherton Press, Inc., 1964).

A. Most Prestigious
   American Political Science Review
B. Considerable Prestige
   World Politics
   Journal of Politics
C. Less Prestigious
   Political Science Quarterly
   Administrative Science Quarterly
   Western Political Quarterly
   Public Administration Review
   Public Opinion Quarterly
   Midwest Journal of Politics
   American Behavioral Science

DESCRIPTION OF TOP JOURNALS

American Political Science Review
(Quarterly) Contains articles on the discipline generally, often reflecting new research developments, and is invaluable for its book reviews, bibliographical articles, notes and lists. This is the official journal of the American Political Science Association.
World Politics
(Quarterly) Published by the Center of International Affairs, Princeton University, it presents articles on international affairs and pertinent book reviews.

Journal of Politics
(Quarterly) Published by the Southern Political Science Association, it carries articles and book reviews on political science in general.

Political Science Quarterly
A journal publishing scholarly essays, research articles, and book reviews, edited by the faculty of the Political Science Department of Columbia University.

Administrative Science Quarterly
Offers academic discussion of public administration, but broadly viewed, giving it utility to political scientists.

Western Political Quarterly
Published by the Institute of Government, University of Utah, this quarterly contains scholarly articles and book reviews of a general character and occasionally gives particular attention to affairs of the American western states.

Public Administration Review
(Quarterly) Published by the American Society for Public Administration, it features general articles, reviews of books and documents and notes on current developments.

Public Opinion Quarterly
Contains research articles on all phases of the subject, with various disciplinary approaches, and book reviews.

Midwest Journal of Political Science
(Quarterly) Carries articles and book reviews ranging over the discipline of political science, published by the Midwest Conference of Political Scientists.

American Behavioral Scientist
(Monthly except July and August) Devoted to short articles on political theory, research, and interdisciplinary studies in the social and behavioral sciences.

CORRESPONDENCE TO GOVERNMENT OFFICIALS

Writing Tips

Rep. Morris K. Udall (Dem., Ariz.) and the League of Women Voters have provided these hints on how to write to a Member of Congress:

Write to your own Senator or Congressman. Letters sent to others will end up on the desk of your representative eventually anyway.

Write at the proper time, when a bill is being discussed in committee or on the floor.

Use your own words and your own stationery. Avoid signing and sending a form or mimeographed letter.

Don't be a pen pal. Don't try to instruct the Representative or Senator on every issue that comes up.

Don't demand a commitment before all the facts are in. Bills rarely become law in the same form as they are introduced.

Identify all bills by their title or their number.

If possible, include pertinent editorials from local papers.

Be constructive. If a bill deals with a problem you admit exists, but you believe the bill is the wrong approach, tell what you think the right approach is.

If you have expert knowledge or wide experience in a particular area, share it with the appropriate person. But don't pretend to wield vast political influence.

Write to a member of Congress when he does something you approve of. A note of appreciation will make him remember you more favorably the next time.

Feel free to write when you have a question or problem dealing with procedures of government departments.

Be brief, write legibly and be sure to use the proper form of address.

Correct Form for Writing to Government Officials

President

> The President
> The White House
> Washington, D. C. 20500
> Dear Mr. President:
> Very respectfully yours,

Vice-President

> The Vice President
> The White House
> Washington, D. C. 20500
> Dear Mr. Vice President:
> Sincerely yours,

Senator

> The Honorable Quentin N. Burdick
> United States Senate
> Washington, D. C. 20510
> Dear Senator Burdick:
> Sincerely yours,

Representative

> The Honorable Leslie C. Arends
> House of Representatives
> Washington, D. C. 20515
> Dear Mr. Arends:
> Sincerely yours,

Member of the Cabinet

> The Honorable Melvin R. Laird
> The Secretary of Defense
> Washington, D. C. 20520
> Dear Mr. Secretary:
> Sincerely yours,

RULES AND TECHNIQUES OF SUCCESSFUL INTERVIEWING

In an effort to become more scientific, political scientists in recent years have begun to use the research technique of the interview to a much greater degree. It is not surprising, therefore, that a great number of undergraduate and graduate students alike have themselves employed this technique.

Due to the fact that this trend is increasing, and in the estimate of the authors, will continue to increase, the following rules are suggested in order that a smooth and successful interview can be accomplished. (The following techniques are paraphrased from the manual for student research projects from the American University's Washington Semester Program.)

1. Try to make an appointment. Do not just "drop in" on a

busy official unless he has invited you to do so, or unless you have been unable to get his office to give you an appointment.

2. Be prompt for appointments. Leave a sufficient safety margin in your travel time to the appointment to cover accidental delays and getting lost.

3. While waiting to be shown in, verify the spelling of the name and title of the official you are going to interview, and the pronunciation of his name, if in doubt. Write these things down for your bibliography and other later uses. Mark down the date of the interview.

4. Ask the secretary, also, for printed materials that might be available.

5. Begin the interview by telling who you are, why you are doing the project, and what it is about.

6. Have several specific questions prepared, covering your purpose for being there. These should be ones which fill necessary gaps remaining in your information after you have done all the reading for the project. These questions may then lead to others.

7. Take notes only with permission, and even then, only if you are sure that doing so will not destroy the usefulness of the interview. Sometimes it is better to wait until the interview is over to take down what was said.

8. Do not quote one official to another!

9. Thank the person interviewed and leave just as soon as you feel that you have the information you need, unless he is clearly not busy and is willing to talk further. Don't overstay your welcome.

10. Write a note of thanks to the person interviewed within a week. This should be regarded as a strict obligation. No single act does more for the benefit of future students seeking similar interviews.

Remember that you are carrying the reputation of your college on your shoulders when interviewing. If you leave behind you a trail of irritation, or if you present yourself ill-prepared, or if you fail to show decent courtesy and gratitude, you will make life that much harder for other students who may come later to interview the same people.

As a final note about interviewing, bear in mind that you are doing serious research. The number of interviews is far less important than the quality of the information gained. Seek out the knowledgeable, not the garrulous, and ask each interviewee for suggestions for future interviews.

NATIONAL AND INTERNATIONAL INTEREST GROUPS

There are countless interest groups with offices in Washington, D.C. that can provide information on their particular concerns. Often a simple postcard is all that is necessary to request information. A more complete listing can be found in *The Encyclopedia of Associations* (Detroit: Gale Research Co., 1968).

African-American Institute
Room 500,
1346 Connecticut Avenue, NW
Washington, D.C.

Air Traffic Control Association
Room 409,
525 School Street, SW
Washington, D.C.

American Association for the Advancement of Science
1515 Massachusetts Avenue
Washington, D.C.

American Association of Junior Colleges
1315 Sixteenth Street, NW
Washington, D.C.

American Council on Education
1785 Massachusetts Avenue, NW
Washington, D.C.

American Farm Bureau Federation
425 Thirteenth Street, NW
Washington, D.C.

American Federation of Labor and Congress of Industrial Organizations
815 Sixteenth Street, NW
Washington, D.C.

American Friends of the Middle East
1605 New Hampshire Avenue, NW
Washington, D.C.

American Institute of Architects
1735 New York Avenue, NW
Washington, D.C.

American Israel Public Affairs Committee
1341 G Street, NW
Washington, D.C.

American Legion
1608 K Street, NW
Washington, D.C.

American Peace Society
4000 Albemarle Street, NW
Washington, D.C.

American Petroleum Institute
1101 Seventeenth Street, NW
Washington, D.C.

American Public Power Association
2600 Virginia Avenue
Washington, D.C.

Americans for Constitutional Action
20 E Street, NW
Washington, D.C.

Americans for Democratic Action
1424 Sixteenth Street, NW
Washington, D.C.

Anti-Communist World Freedom Congress, Inc.
1221 Massachusetts Avenue, NW
Washington, D.C.

American Veterans Committee
1333 Connecticut Avenue, NW
Washington, D.C.

Chamber of Commerce of the U.S.
1615 H Street, NW
Washington, D.C.

Chiefs of Police, International
Association of
1319 Eighteenth Street, NW
Washington, D.C.

Civil Liberties Union
1424 Sixteenth Street, NW
Washington, D.C.

Council of Graduate Schools of
the U.S.
1785 Massachusetts Avenue, NW
Washington, D.C.

Council of State Governments
1735 DeSales Street, NW
Washington, D.C.

Defense Supply Association
1026 Seventeenth Street, NW
Washington, D.C.

Distilled Spirits Institute
425 Thirteenth Street, NW
Washington, D.C.

Fair Campaign Practices
Committee
328 Pennsylvania Avenue, S.E.
Washington, D.C.

Society of American Foresters
919 Seventeenth Street, NW
Washington, D.C.

Home Study Council, National
1601 Eighteenth Street, NW
Washington, D.C.

League of Women Voters of the
United States
1200 Seventeenth Street, NW
Washington, D.C.

National Association for the
Advancement of Colored People
422 First Street, SE
Washington, D.C.

National Association of Daughters
of the American Revolution
1776 D Street, NW
Washington, D.C.

National Association of Social
Workers
1346 Connecticut Avenue, NW
Washington, D.C.

National Committee against
Mental Illness
1028 Connecticut Avenue, NW
Washington, D.C.

National Confederation of
American Ethnic Groups
1629 K Street, NW
Washington, D.C.

National Council of Negro Women
1346 Connecticut Avenue, NW
Washington, D.C.

National Democratic Committee
2600 Virginia Avenue, NW
Washington, D.C.

National Farmers Union
1012 Fourteenth Street, NW
Washington, D.C.

National Grange
1616 H Street, NW
Washington, D.C.

National Guard Association of
the U.S.
One Massachusetts Avenue, NW
Washington, D.C.

National Rifle Association of
America
1600 Rhode Island Avenue, NW
Washington, D.C.

National Rivers and Harbors
Congress
1028 Connecticut Avenue, NW
Washington, D.C.

National Sheriff's Association
1250 Connecticut Avenue, NW
Washington, D.C.

Navy League of the U.S.
818 Eighteenth Street, NW
Washington, D.C.

Peanut Council, National
1120 Connecticut Avenue, NW
Washington, D.C.

Pharmaceutical Manufacturers
1155 Fifteenth Street, NW
Washington, D.C.

Right-to-Work Committee
1900 L Street, NW
Washington, D.C.

Student Nonviolent Coordinating
   Committee
2208 Fourteenth Street, NW
Washington, D.C.

Taxpayers Association, American
425 Thirteenth Street, NW
Washington, D.C.

The Urban Coalition
1819 H Street, NW
Washington, D.C.

United Nations Association of the
   USA
1325 Massachusetts Avenue, NW
Washington, D.C.

United States Army, Association
   of the
1529 Eighteenth Street, NW
Washington, D.C.

United World Federalist
2029 K Street, NW
Washington, D.C.

Young Democratic Clubs of
   America
2600 Virginia Avenue, NW
Washington, D.C.

Young Republican National
   Federation
1625 First Street, NW
Washington, D.C.

World Wildlife Fund
910 Seventeenth Street, NW
Washington, D.C.

INFORMATION SERVICES IN THE UNITED STATES
OF MEMBERS OF THE UNITED NATIONS

Like interest groups, nation-states are quite eager to provide information on their governments and policies. Therefore the following information services are provided.

Afghanistan
Embassy of Afghanistan
2001 Twenty-fourth Street
Washington, D.C.

Albania
Permanent Mission of the
   People's Republic of Albania
   to the UN
446 East Eighty-sixth Street
New York, N.Y.

Algeria
Permanent Mission of Algeria
   to the UN
750 Third Avenue
New York, N.Y.

Argentina
Embassy of the Argentine
   Republic
1600 New Hampshire Avenue,
   NW
Washington, D.C.

Australia
Australian News and Information Bureau
636 Fifth Avenue
New York, N.Y.

Austria
Austrian Information Service
31 East Sixty-ninth Street
New York, N.Y.

Barbados
Barbados Tourist and Development Board
801 Second Avenue
New York, N.Y.

Belgium
Belgian Consulate General
50 Rockefeller Plaza
New York, N.Y.

Bolivia
Embassy of Bolivia
1145 Nineteenth Street, NW
Washington, D.C.

Botswana
Permanent Mission of
Botswana to the UN
Room 511
866 United Nations Plaza
New York, N.Y.

Brazil
Brazilian Government Trade
Bureau
551 Fifth Avenue
New York, N.Y.

Bulgaria
Embassy of the People's
Republic of Bulgaria
2100 Sixteenth Street, NW
Washington, D.C.

Burma
Consulate General of Burma
10 East Seventy-seventh Street
New York, N.Y.

Burundi
Permanent Mission of the
Kingdom of Burundi to the
UN
485 Fifth Avenue
New York, N.Y.

Byelorussian Soviet Socialist
Republic
See Union of Soviet Socialist
Republics

Cambodia
Permanent Mission of
Cambodia to the UN
845 Third Avenue
New York, N.Y.

Cameroon
Permanent Mission of the
Federal Republic of
Cameroon to the UN
Room 650
866 United Nations Plaza
New York, N.Y.

Canada
Consulate General of Canada
Press and Information Service
680 Fifth Avenue
New York, N.Y.

Central African Republic
Permanent Mission of the
Central African Republic to
the UN
Room 1614
386 Park Avenue South
New York, N.Y.

Ceylon
Embassy of Ceylon
2148 Wyoming Avenue, NW
Washington, D.C.

Chad
Permanent Mission of the
Republic of Chad to the UN
Apt. 5C
150 East Fifty-second Street
New York, N.Y.

Chile
Consulate General of Chile
809 United Nations Plaza
New York, N.Y.

China
Chinese Information Service
100 West Thirty-second Street
New York, N.Y.

Colombia
Consulate General of Colombia
10 East Forty-sixth Street
New York, N.Y.

Congo (Brazzaville)
Permanent Mission of the
  Republic of the Congo
  (Brazzaville) to the UN
Room 1604
444 Madison Avenue
New York, N.Y.

Congo Democratic Republic
Permanent Mission of the
  Democratic Republic of the
  Congo to the UN
402 East Fifty-first Street
New York, N.Y.

Costa Rica
Permanent Mission of Costa
  Rica to the UN
Room 2002
211 East Forty-third Street
New York, N.Y.

Cuba
Permanent Mission of Cuba
  to the UN
6 East Sixty-seventh Street
New York, N.Y.

Cyprus
Permanent Mission of Cyprus
  to the UN
Apt. 19J
165 East Seventy-second Street
New York, N.Y.

Czechoslovakia
Embassy of the Czechoslovak
  Republic
2349 Massachusetts Avenue NW
Washington, D.C.

Dahomey
Permanent Mission of the
  Republic of Dahomey to the
  UN
4 East Seventy-third Street
New York, N.Y.

Denmark
Danish Consulate General
280 Park Avenue
New York, N.Y.

Dominican Republic
Permanent Mission of the
  Dominican Republic to the
  UN
144 East Forty-fourth Street
New York, N.Y.

Ecuador
Consulate General of Ecuador
1270 Avenue of the Americas
New York, N.Y.

El Salvador
Consulate General of
  El Salvador
211 East Forty-third Street
New York, N.Y.

Ethiopia
Embassy of Ethiopia
2134 Kalorama Road, NW
Washington, D.C.

Finland
Finnish Consulate General
200 East Forty-second Street
New York, N.Y.

France
Embassy of France
972 Fifth Avenue
New York, N.Y.

Gabon
Permanent Mission of the
 Republic of Gabon to the UN
Room 536
866 United Nations Plaza
New York, N.Y.

Gambia
Permanent Mission of Gambia
 to the UN
c/o Mission of Senegal
51 East Forty-second Street
New York, N.Y.

Ghana
Ghana Information and Trade
 Center
565 Fifth Avenue
New York, N.Y.

Greece
Greek Consulate General
69 East Seventy-ninth Street
New York, N.Y.

Guatemala
Consulate General of Guatemala
1270 Avenue of the Americas
New York, N.Y.

Guinea
Embassy of Guinea
2112 Leroy Place, NW
Washington 8, D.C.

Guyana
Permanent Mission of Guyana
 to the UN
355 Lexington Avenue
New York, N.Y.

Haiti
Consulate of Haiti
60 East Forty-second Street
New York, N.Y.

Honduras
Permanent Mission of
 Honduras to the UN
Room 603
290 Madison Avenue
New York, N.Y.

Hungary
Permanent Mission of the
 Hungarian People's Republic
 to the UN
10 East Seventy-fifth Street
New York, N.Y.

Iceland
Consulate General of Iceland
420 Lexington Avenue
New York, N.Y.

India
Indian Consulate General
3 East Sixty-fourth Street
New York, N.Y.

Indonesia
Consulate General of
 Indonesia
5 East sixty-eighth Street
New York, N.Y.

Iran
Consulate General of Iran
630 Fifth Avenue
New York, N.Y.

Iraq
Permanent Mission of Iraq
 to the UN
c/o Press Officer
14 East Seventy-ninth Street
New York, N.Y.

Ireland
Consulate General of Ireland
33 East Fiftieth Street
New York, N.Y.

Israel
The Israel Office of
 Information
11 East Seventieth Street
New York, N.Y.

Italy
Italian Cultural Institute
686 Park Avenue
New York, N.Y.

Ivory Coast
Permanent Mission of Ivory
    Coast to the UN
46 East Seventy-fourth Street
New York, N.Y.

Jamaica
Consulate General of Jamaica
Information Service
200 Park Avenue
New York, N.Y.

Japan
Japan Information Service
Consulate General of Japan
235 East Forty-second Street
New York, N.Y.

Jordan
Embassy of Jordan
2319 Wyoming Avenue, NW
Washington, D.C.

Kenya
Permanent Mission of the
    Republic of Kenya to the UN
Room 486
866 United Nations Plaza
New York, N.Y.

Kuwait
Permanent Mission of Kuwait
    to the UN
235 East Forty-second Street
New York, N.Y.

Laos
Embassy of Laos
2222 S Street, NW
Washington, D.C.

Lebanon
Consulate General of Lebanon
9 East Seventy-sixth Street
New York, N.Y.

Liberia
Consulate General of Liberia
1120 Avenue of the Americas
New York, N.Y.

Libya
Embassy of Libya
2344 Massachusetts Avenue, NW
Washington, D.C.

Luxembourg
Consulate General of
    Luxembourg
200 East Forty-second Street
New York, N.Y.

Madagascar
Permanent Mission of the
    Malagasy Republic to the UN
Embassy House, Apt. 2H
301 East Forty-seventh Street
New York, N.Y.

Malawi
Permanent Mission of the
    Republic of Malawi to the
    UN
777 Third Avenue
New York, N.Y.

Malaysia
Permanent Mission of
    Malaysia to the UN
845 Third Avenue
New York, N.Y.

Mali
Permanent Mission of the
    Republic of Mali to the UN
111 East Sixty-ninth Street
New York, N.Y.

Malta
Permanent Mission of Malta
    to the UN
155 East Forty-fourth Street
New York, N.Y.

Mauritania
Permanent Mission of the
    Islamic Republic of
    Mauritania to the UN
8 West Fortieth Street
New York, N.Y.

Mauritius
Permanent Mission of
Mauritius to the UN
Apt. 3C
301 East Forty-seventh Street
New York, N.Y.

Mexico
Mexican Consulate General
8 East Forty-first Street
New York, N.Y.

Mongolia
Permanent Mission of the
Mongolian People's Republic
to the UN
6 East Seventy-seventh Street
New York, N.Y.

Morocco
Embassy of Morocco
1601 Twenty-first Street, NW
Washington, D.C.

Nepal
Royal Nepalese Consulate
General
300 East Forty-sixth Street
New York, N.Y.

Netherlands
Netherlands Information Service
711 Third Avenue
New York, N.Y.

New Zealand
Consulate General of New
Zealand
630 Fifth Avenue
New York, N.Y.

Nicaragua
Consulate General of Nicaragua
Room 1818
1270 Avenue of the Americas
New York, N.Y.

Niger
Permanent Mission of Niger
to the UN
Suite 570
866 United Nations Plaza
New York, N.Y.

Nigeria
Permanent Mission of Nigeria
to the UN
757 Third Avenue
New York, N.Y.

Norway
Norwegian Information Service
290 Madison Avenue
New York, N.Y.

Pakistan
Permanent Mission of
Pakistan to the UN
8 East Sixty-fifth Street
New York, N.Y.

Panama
Consulate General of Panama
1270 Avenue of the Americas
New York, N.Y.

Paraguay
Permanent Mission of
Paraguay to the UN
32 Broadway
New York, N.Y.

Peru
Consulate General of Peru
10 Rockefeller Plaza
New York, N.Y.

Philippines
Consulate General of the
Philippines
15 East Sixty-sixth Street
New York, N.Y.

Poland
Embassy of the Polish People's
Republic
2224 Wyoming Avenue, NW
Washington, D.C.

Portugal
Casa de Portugal
570 Fifth Avenue
New York, N.Y.

Rumania
Embassy of the Socialist
  Republic of Rumania
160 Twenty-third Street, NE
Washington, D.C.

Rwanda
Permanent Mission of the
  Rwandese Republic to the UN
Room 630
120 East Fifty-sixth Street
New York, N.Y.

Saudi Arabia
Saudi Arabian Consulate
  General
Room 527
866 United Nations Plaza
New York, N.Y.

Senegal
Permanent Mission of the
  Republic of Senegal to the UN
51 East Forty-second Street
New York, N.Y.

Sierra Leone
Consulate General of Sierra
  Leone
Room 609
30 East Forty-second Street
New York, N.Y.

Singapore
Permanent Mission of
  Singapore to the UN
711 Third Avenue
New York, N.Y.

Somalia
Permanent Mission of
  Somalia to the UN
236 East Forty-sixth Street
New York, N.Y.

South Africa
South African Information
  Service
655 Madison Avenue
New York, N.Y.

Southern Yemen
Permanent Mission of the
  People's Republic of Southern
  Yemen to the UN
Room 427
866 United Nations Plaza
New York, N.Y.

Spain
Embassy of Spain
Office of the Cultural
  Counselor
2700 Fifteenth Street, NW
Washington, D.C.

Sudan
Permanent Mission of the
  Republic of Sudan to the UN
757 Third Avenue
New York, N.Y.

Swaziland
Permanent Mission of the
  Kingdom of Swaziland to the
  United Nations
141 East Forty-fourth Street
New York, N.Y.

Sweden
Swedish Information Service
825 Third Avenue
New York, N.Y.

Syria
Permanent Mission of the
  Syrian Arab Republic to the
  UN
Room 2505
757 Third Avenue
New York, N.Y.

Thailand
Embassy of Thailand
2300 Kalorama Road
Washington, D.C.

Togo
Permanent Mission of Togo to
  the UN
Room 400
801 Second Avenue
New York, N.Y.

Trinidad and Tobago
Embassy of Trinidad and Tobago
2209 Massachusetts Avenue
Washington, D.C.

Tunisia
Trade and Tourist Office
Room 2918
Pan Am Building
200 Park Avenue
New York, N.Y.

Turkey
Turkish Government Tourism
    and Information Office
500 fifth Avenue
New York, N.Y.

Uganda
Permanent Mission of Uganda
    to the UN
801 Second Avenue
New York, N.Y.

Ukrainian Soviet Socialist
    Republic
See Union of Soviet Socialist
    Republics

Union of Soviet Socialist
    Republics
Permanent Mission of Union
    of Soviet Socialist Republics
    to the UN
136 East Sixty-seventh Street
New York, N.Y.

United Arab Republic
Permanent Mission of United
    Arab Republic to the UN
36 East Sixty-seventh Street
New York, N.Y.

United Kingdom
British Information Services
845 Third Avenue
New York, N.Y.

United Republic of Tanzania
Permanent Mission of the
    United Republic of Tanzania
Room 1300
205 East Forty-second Street
New York, N.Y.

United States
Department of State
Public Services Division
Washington, D.C.

Upper Volta
Permanent Mission of the
    Republic of Upper Volta
    to the UN
236 East Forty-sixth Street
New York, N.Y.

Uruguay
Consulate General of Uruguay
17 Battery Place
New York, N.Y.

Venezuela
Consulate General of
    Venezuela
600 Fifth Avenue
New York, N.Y.

Yemen
Permanent Mission of the Arab
    Republic of Yemen to the UN
211 East Forty-third Street
New York, N.Y.

Yugoslavia
Yugoslavia Information Center
816 Fifth Avenue
New York, N.Y.

Zambia
Permanent Mission of the
    Republic of Zambia
641 Lexington Avenue
New York, N.Y.

INFORMATION SERVICES OF ACCREDITED
OBSERVERS AND NONMEMBER STATES
IN THE UNITED NATIONS

Germany (Federal Republic)
German Consulate General
460 Park Avenue
New York, N.Y.

Holy See
Office of the Permanent
   Observer of the Holy See to
   the UN
c/o Holy Family Church
315 East Forty-seventh Street
New York, N.Y.

Korea
Consulate General of Korea
9 East Eightieth Street
New York, N.Y.

Monaco
Monaco Information Center
610 Fifth Avenue
New York, N.Y.

Switzerland
Consulate General of
   Switzerland
444 Madison Avenue
New York, N.Y.

Vietnam
Office of the Permanent
   Observer of Vietnam to
   the UN
866 United Nations Plaza
New York, N.Y.

THE LIBRARY CARD CATALOG

Practically every library in the United States uses one of two
classification systems — the Dewey decimal classification or the
Library of Congress classification. These two classification
systems differ in their approach; an explanation of each follows.

Dewey Decimal Classification

Melvil Dewey worked out this approach in the latter part of the
nineteenth century. The Dewey decimal classification system
divides all knowledge, as represented by books and other materials
which are acquired by libraries, into nine main classes which
are numbered by digits 1 to 9. Material too general to belong to
any one of these classes, such as newspapers and encyclopedias,
falls into a tenth class, numbered 0, which precedes the others.
The classes are written as hundreds; thus, 000 is general works,
100 is philosophy, 200 is religion, 300 social sciences, and so
on. Each division is again divided into nine sections preceded by
a general section; thus, 300 is social science in general, while
321 is forms of state, 322 the state and religion, 323 the relationship
between states and individuals or groups, etc. Further division to

bring together like materials is accomplished by the addition of digits following a decimal point. Usually, most numbers do not exceed six digits in length, i.e., three to the right of the decimal point; however, there are cases of numbers extending to nine and sometimes even more digits.

The basic classification system ranges from 000 to 999:

000—099	General works
100—199	Philosophy
200—299	Religion
300—399	Social sciences
400—499	Language
500—599	Pure sciences
600—699	Technology
700—799	Arts
800—899	Literature
900—999	History

The broad category of most relevance to political scientists is 300-399 the social sciences.

300—309	The social sciences, general
310—319	Statistics
320—329	Political science
330—339	Economics
340—349	Law
350—359	Public administration
360—369	Social welfare
370—379	Education
380—389	Public services and utilities
390—399	Customs and folklore

The specific category of most relevance to this study is that of "political science" (320—329) which is broken down into ten subclasses, each of which may be further subdivided by the use of decimals. For example, the subclass 326, "slavery," then becomes 326.1, "slave trade," 326.2, "coolies and contract slaves," 326.3, "serfs and serfdom," etc.

320	Political science, general
321	Forms of states
322	State and church
323	State and individual

324   Suffrage and elections
325   Migration and colonization
326   Slavery
327   Foreign relations
328   Legislation
329   Political parties

For the complete list of subclassifications see the *Dewey Decimal Classification and Relative Index*, 18th ed. 2 vols. (New York: Forest Press, Inc., of Lake Placid Club Education Foundation, 1970).

Library of Congress Classification

The Library of Congress classification system was adopted in 1900, three years after the Library of Congress moved from the capitol to its new building. It changed systems in order to have a more systematic and functional arrangement of the Library's collection.

This system divided the fields of knowledge into twenty groups by assigning a letter to each and combining arabic numerals and additional letters to separate the main groups into classes and subclasses in somewhat of a similar way used in the Dewey decimal system. All books are divided into the following basic groups:

A	General works	M	Music
B	Philosophy and religion	N	Fine arts
C	History and auxiliary sciences	P	Language and literature
		Q	Science
D	Foreign history and topography	R	Medicine
		S	Agriculture
E-F	American history	T	Technology
G	Geography and anthropology	U	Military science
H	Social science	V	Naval science
J	Political science	Z	Bibliography and library science
K	Law		
L	Education		

For political scientists, class J (political science) is the most relevant. Within each class subdivisions are denoted by a second letter. Thus for political science, we have the following subclasses:

J Official documents
JA General works
JC Political theory
JF Constitutional history and administration
JK United States
JL British America, Latin America
JN Europe
JQ Asia, Africa, Australia, Pacific Islands
JS Local government
JV Colonies and colonization
JX International law and international relations

Each subclass makes up several smaller regional, historical, or functional subdivisions. For the complete list of subclassifications see *Classification: Class J, Political Science*, 2nd ed. (Washington, D.C.: Government Printing Office, 1924; reprinted in 1966).

HOW TO FIND UNITED STATES STATUTES AND UNITED STATES CODE CITATIONS

The following chart, (Table 5), drawn up by the House Judiciary Committee will help in obtaining, quickly and easily, an up-to-date and accurate citation to the *United States Statutes at Large* and the *United States Code.* In using the chart, the reader should read the items from left to right across the page.

The first column contains the typical references which require further citing, which are the Revised Statutes section; date of law; name of law; number of law; Statutes citation; and Code citation. The second, third, and fourth columns point to the official published volumes in which the citations may be found and suggest logical sequences to follow in making the search. Column five suggests additional finding aids, some of which especially are useful for citing current legislation, and the last column shows some examples of the citations resulting from following the steps in the chart. A careful following of the steps set forth carries the assurance that each search will be complete and that all appropriate points will be covered.

Publications referred to in abbreviated form are identified and described in a list at the end.

HOW TO FIND CITATIONS TO THE UNITED
THE UNITED

IF YOU HAVE this reference—	AND YOU USE THESE basic finding aids—	
	U.S. STATUTES AT LARGE (new volume added each year)	U.S. CODE [1] (new edition each 6 years)
1. Revised Statutes Section ___ [e.g., Rev. Stat. 56]	[Revised Statutes, 1873, were published as pt. 1, vol. 18, U.S. Statutes at Large; 2d edition published in 1878.]	Use U.S.C. tables volume to find U.S.C. section; verify text; then—
2. Date of Law: [2] (a) For any year *up to* and *through* year of last edition of U.S.C.; [e.g., June 23, 1947]	Use Stat. volume for that year to check the List of Public Laws; get law number and verify page number from List; then—	Use U.S.C. tables volume to find U.S.C. section; verify text; then—
(b) For any year *after* year of last edition of U.S.C. and *through* year of latest Supplement;	Use Stat. volume for that year to check the List of Public Laws; get law number and verify page number from List; then—	----------------------------
(c) For current year ___	----------------------------	----------------------------
3. Name of Law: (a) For any year *up to* and *through* year of last edition of U.S.C.; [e.g., Federal Register Act.].	----------------------------	Use U.S.C. popular names index (preceding general index) to obtain Stat. and U.S.C. citations; verify both; then—
(b) For any year *after* year of last edition of U.S.C. and *through* year of latest Supplement;	----------------------------	----------------------------
(c) For current year ___	----------------------------	----------------------------

See footnotes at end of table, p. 6.

STATES STATUTES AT LARGE AND TO STATES CODE

PLUS latest published— U.S. CODE SUPPLEMENT (*all* changes since last edition)	AND/OR THESE additional finding aids— (See "REFERENCES" at end of pamphlet)	YOU SHOULD GET this citation—
Check latest U.S.C. Supplement for recent changes; verify text.	Check Table 3 in latest U.S.C. Cong. & Adm. News for changes during current period; if Code section is included, verify text in same publication or in slip law.	Rev. Stat. 56. 2 U.S.C. 64.
Check latest U.S.C. Supplement for recent changes; verify text.	Check Table 3 in latest U.S.C. Cong. & Adm. News for changes during current period; if Code section is included, verify text in same publication or in slip law.	61 Stat. 136. 29 U.S.C. 141–197.
Use tables volume in latest U.S.C. Supplement to find U.S.C. section; verify text.	Check Table 3 in latest U.S.C. Cong. & Adm. News for changes during current period; if Code section is included, verify text in same publication or in slip law. Use slip law or U.S.C. Cong. & Adm. News *text* to get law number and Stat. citation and to verify subject matter; then use Table 2, U.S.C. Cong. & Adm. News to find U.S.C. classification.	
Check latest U.S.C. Supplement for recent changes; verify text.		
Use U.S.C. popular names index (preceding general index) to obtain Stat. and U.S.C. citation; verify both; then—	Check Table 3 in latest U.S.C. Cong. & Adm. News for changes during current period; verify any changes in same publication or in slip law. Other sources: Index of Popular Names in U.S. Statutes at Large *Tables of Laws Affected, 1956–60;* Digest of U.S. Supreme Court Reports; Shepard's Federal Acts by Popular Names or Short Titles; U.S.C.A. Popular Name Table; FCA tables volume.	49 Stat. 500. 44 U.S.C. 301–314.
	Use House Calendar *index* and *numerical list* to get bill number, then law number (if assigned); or U.S.C. Cong. & Adm. News *index* or Table 10; use slip law or U.S.C. Cong. & Adm. News *text* to get Stat. citation and to verify date and subject matter; then, with law number, use Table 2, U.S.C. Cong. & Adm. News to find U.S.C. classification.	

HOW TO FIND CITATIONS TO THE UNITED
THE UNITED

IF YOU HAVE this reference—	AND YOU USE THESE basic finding aids—	
	U.S. STATUTES AT LARGE (new volume added each year)	U.S. CODE [1] (new edition each 6 years)
4. Number of Law:		
(a) For any year *up to* and *through* year of last edition of U.S.C. and the law—		
(1) *does not* have a numerical prefix; [e.g., Public Law 706]	[You will need additional information, such as the Congress, the year, or the Stat. volume; then] use the Stat. volume to check the List of Public Laws; get and verify page number from List; then—	Use U.S.C. tables volume to find U.S.C. section; verify text; then—
(2) *does* have a numerical prefix; [e.g., Public Law 85–227]	Use Stat. volume for the Congress indicated by the numerical prefix; check the List of Public Laws; get and verify page number from List; then—	Use U.S.C. tables volume to find U.S.C. section; verify text; then—
(b) For any year *after* last edition of U.S.C. and *through* year of latest Supplement; [e.g., Public Law 89–99]	Use Stat. volume for the Congress indicated by the numerical prefix; check the List of Public Laws; get and verify page number from List; then—	
(c) For current year		
5. Stat. Citation: [3]		
(a) For any year *up to* and *through* year of last edition of U.S.C.; [e.g., 72 Stat. 997]	Use Stat. volume to get date and law number; verify subject matter, then—	Use U.S.C. tables volume to find U.S.C. section; verify text; then—
(b) For any year *after* year of last edition of U.S.C. and *through* year of latest Supplement;	Use Stat. volume to get date and law number; verify subject matter; then—	
(c) For current year		

See footnotes at end of table, p. 6.

STATES STATUTES AT LARGE AND TO STATES CODE—Continued

PLUS latest published— U.S. CODE SUPPLEMENT (*all* changes since last edition)	AND/OR THESE additional finding aids— (See "REFERENCES" at end of pamphlet)	YOU SHOULD GET this citation—
Check latest U.S.C. Supplement for recent changes; verify text.	Check Table 3 in latest U.S.C. Cong. & Adm. News for changes during current period; if Code section is included, verify text in same publication or in slip law.	60 Stat. 968. 25 U.S.C. 601–607.
Check latest U.S.C. Supplement for recent changes; verify text.	Check Table 3 in latest U.S.C. Cong. & Adm. News for changes during current period; if Code section is included, verify text in same publication or in slip law.	71 Stat. 512. 42 U.S.C. 418 and note.
Use tables volume in latest U.S.C. Supplement to find U.S.C. section; verify text.	Check Table 3 in latest U.S.C. Cong. & Adm. News for changes during current period; if Code section is included, verify text in same publication or in slip law.	79 Stat. 424. 46 U.S.C. 441–445.
- - - - - - - - - - - - - - - - - - - -	Use slip law or U.S.C. Cong. & Adm. News *text* to get Stat. citation and to verify date and subject matter; then, with law number, use Table 2, U.S.C. Cong. & Adm. News to find U.S.C. classification.	
Check latest U.S.C. Supplement for recent changes; verify text; then—	Check Table 3 in latest U.S.C. Cong. & Adm. News for changes during current period; if Code section is included, verify text in same publication or in slip law.	72 Stat. 997. 29 U.S.C. 301–309.
Use tables volume in latest U.S.C. Supplement to find U.S.C. section; verify text; then— -	Check Table 3 in latest U.S.C. Cong. & Adm. News for changes during current period; if Code section is included, verify text in same publication or in slip law. Use slip law or U.S.C. Cong. & Adm. News *text* to verify subject matter, date, and law number. Table 2, U.S.C. Cong. & Adm. News may be used to find U.S.C. classification.	

HOW TO FIND CITATIONS TO THE UNITED
THE UNITED

IF YOU HAVE this reference—	AND YOU USE THESE basic finding aids—	
	U.S. STATUTES AT LARGE (new volume added each year)	U.S. CODE [1] (new edition each 6 years)
6. U.S.C. Citation:		
(a) For any year *up to* and *through* year of last edition of U.S.C.; [e.g., 5 U.S.C. 630d]	--------------------------------	Check section in U.S.C. to verify subject matter and determine appropriate Stat. citation; verify text against Stat. volume; then—
(b) For any year *after* year of last edition of U.S.C. and *through* year of latest supplement;	--------------------------------	--------------------------------
(c) For current year	--------------------------------	--------------------------------

[1] If U.S. Code is not available, use U.S.C.A. or F.C.A. and their supplements.

[2] You will need some knowledge of the subject matter if more than one law was signed on the same day.

[3] You will need some knowledge of the subject matter if more than one law appears on the same page.

STATES STATUTES AT LARGE AND TO
STATES CODE—Continued

PLUS latest published— U.S. CODE SUPPLEMENT (*all* changes since last edition)	AND/OR THESE additional finding aids— (See "REFERENCES" at end of pamphlet)	YOU SHOULD GET this citation—
Check latest U.S.C. Supplement for recent changes; verify text; then—	Check Table 3 in latest U.S.C. Cong. & Adm. News for changes during current period; if Code section is included, verify text in same publication or in slip law.	63 Stat. 381. 5 U.S.C. 630d.
Check section in latest U.S.C. Supplement to verify subject matter and determine appropriate Stat. citation; verify text against Stat. volume; then— --------------------------------	Check Table 3 in latest U.S.C. Cong. & Adm. News for changes during current period; if Code section is included, verify text in same publication or in slip law. Check Table 3 in latest U.S.C. Cong. & Adm. News; if Code section is included, get page number on which text of law appears, get law number from that page (footnote should show Code citation there), then get specific Stat. citation from slip law and verify subject matter.	

REFERENCES

Title	Description
Government Publications:	
1. Slip law_____	A pamphlet print, complete with annotations and legislative history, of each public and private law enacted by Congress; issued within a few days after bill is signed by the President; text form later cumulated and bound, with finding aids, as Stat. volume.
2. Stat_____	United States Statutes at Large; contains all public and private laws and concurrent resolutions enacted during a session of Congress, plus reorganization plans, proposed and ratified amendments to the Constitution, and proclamations by the President; arrangement is chronological by approval date in each category; by law, these volumes are "legal evidence" (1 U.S.C. 112); only the general and permanent laws are codified (arranged by subject in titles) in the U.S.C.
3. Tables of Laws Affected_____	Since 1956, tables of prior laws affected each year published for each Statutes volume; the first 5-year cumulation (1956-60) of these tables issued as a separate 233-page booklet; the 10-year cumulation (1956-65) available in early 1966.
4. Index Analysis of Federal Statutes, 1789-1873; Index to Federal Statutes, 1874-1931.	Subject index covering all general and permanent laws through 46 Stat. (Mar. 4, 1931); useful for tracing early legislation.
5. U.S.C._____	United States Code and its annual, cumulative Supplements; only the general and permanent laws of the United States are codified (arranged by subject in titles) in the U.S. Code; temporary, local, or private laws are not included; the code establishes "prima facie the laws of the United States" except "whenever titles of such Code shall have been enacted into positive law the text thereof shall be legal evidence" (1 U.S.C. 204(a)); to date, 17 titles have been enacted into positive law.
6. U.S.C. Supplement_____	Annual, cumulative supplements to the United States Code; contains all changes in or additions to the general and permanent laws since the last edition of the Code.
7. House Calendar_____	Calendars of the U.S. House of Representatives and History of Legislation (1 publication)—very useful for following day-to-day progress of legislation through both Houses of Congress; index, usually on Mondays; final edition covers the session (1st) or the Congress (end of 2d session).
Non-Government Publications:	
8. U.S.C. Cong. and Adm. News_	United States Code Congressional and Administrative News— published semimonthly during each session of Congress; monthly when Congress is not in session. Gives slip law information, including legislative history; has subject index, list of popular name acts, tables; material is currently supplemental to and annually codified in U.S.C.A.
9. U.S.C.A. and pocket parts_____	United States Code Annotated—an annotated version of the U.S. Code—and annual, cumulative pocket parts.
10. FCA and supplements_____	Federal Code Annotated and supplements—an annotated version of the U.S. Code with monthly, then cumulative, annual supplements.
11. Shepard's popular names_____	Shepard's Federal Acts by Popular Names or Short Title—a pamphlet, supplemented in Shepard's Citations; reissued intermittently.

CONGRESSIONAL RECORD—A DAILY PUBLISHED TRIUMPH ON CONGRESS' DOORSTEP
(Used with permission from Congressional Quarterly Weekly Report, November 28, 1969)

After each daily session of Congress, the Government Printing Office (GPO) publishes the *Congressional Record*— the official report of Congressional proceedings.

About 49,000 copies of the *Record*, averaging more than 200 pages a copy, are produced and delivered by 8 a.m. the following day.

The *Record* is produced in less than 13 hours and involves the efforts of about 2,500 of the GPO's 8,200 employees.

This Fact Sheet describes the effort that goes into the printing of the *Record* and provides information and background on its history and content.

Background

The proceedings of Congress were not printed systematically before 1865, when the *Congressional Globe*—the forerunner of the *Congressional Record*—took on a form and style that later became standard for the *Record*.

According to a 1959 Legislative Reference Service research paper on the *Congressional Record*, "Before 1825, debates in the House of Representatives were not reported except in a haphazard way in some of the better newspapers." The Senate debates, the report said, seldom were reported at all.

Not until 1855 were reporters of Congressional proceedings and debates paid at public expense, and only in 1863 were annual appropriations established in both houses of Congress for reporting proceedings.

When the Government contract for publication of the *Congressional Globe* expired in 1873, Congress passed an appropriations act which provided that with the 43rd Congress (March 4, 1873) the *Congressional Record* would be produced by the GPO.

Contents of the Record

The *Congressional Record* chronologically reports daily what is said on the floor of both houses of Congress. Biweekly and hard-bound versions are also produced to provide a corrected and permanent record. The proceedings of the House and Senate alternately appear first in each daily printing of the Record. The *Record* contains four separate sections:

Proceedings of the House.
Proceedings of the Senate.
Extensions of Remarks.
Daily Digest—a summary of the proceedings in both houses, including a calendar of committee meetings for the following day.

At the beginning of each month a resume of Congressional activity is printed in the *Record*, providing statistical data for the preceeding month on the following:

Days Congress was in session.
Page numbers of proceedings printed in the *Record*.
Page numbers of extensions of remarks.
Bills enacted into law.
Measures reported by committees.
Reports, quorum calls, votes and bills vetoed by the President.
The summary also provides information on the status of Executive nominations.

Proceedings. Although the Record purports to print an exact account of the proceedings on the floor of both chambers, Members of the Senate and the House edit and revise their remarks before they are published.

Proceedings in both the Senate and the House are taken down by separate staffs of reporters, eight in the Senate and seven in the House. The shorthand notes of the debates are read later into a Dictaphone and typed by a transcriber. The typed copy is then proofread by the reporters, given an appropriate heading and sent to the members for their own editing and correction.

Reporting in the House is done on a half-hour schedule, requiring that each reporter spend five minutes of each half hour on the floor and the remaining time dictating, transcribing and correcting his notes. The Senate operates under the same procedures, but on an hourly basis. Each Senate reporter spends 10 minutes of each hour on the floor.

Corrected transcripts of debates must be returned to the GPO by 9 p.m. the same day if they are to be included in the following day's *Record*.

Extensions of Remarks.   Following the record of floor debate in the two houses is a section for Senators and Representatives to extend their remarks—to add to the *Record* materials not actually presented on the floor. Senators may add extraneous material—such as speeches given outside Congress, selected editorials, magazine articles or letters—to the body of the *Record.* Representatives must place such material in the Extensions of Remarks section.

Daily Digest.   The 1946 Congressional Reorganization Act directed the Joint Committee on Printing, which controls the publication of the *Congressional Record*, to incorporate into the *Record* a list of Congressional committee meetings and hearings, their places and subject matter. This section of the *Record,* titled the "Daily Digest," summarizes the following material:
Highlights of the day's Congressional activities.
Senate action.
Senate committee meetings.
House action.
House committee meetings.
Joint committee meetings.
The Daily Digest also lists the committee meetings scheduled the day the *Record* is distributed.
Friday issues of the *Record* contain a section outlining the Congressional program for the coming week, including schedules of major floor action and of House and Senate committee meetings.

Index.   Published semimonthly, the index is the key to using the *Congressional Record.* It is a guide to the contents and means of tracing floor action on legislation.
The index consists of two parts: an index to the proceedings, which includes material both in the body and in the Extension of Remarks section, and an index to the history of bills and resolutions.
Remarks made in heated debates may be judged offensive and edited out by a reporter or the member who made them. Grammar is often improved and the transcripts are often polished.
In the 1950s, Members of Congress frequently inserted into the transcripts of their own remarks such words as "laughter" and "applause." Such additions have become infrequent. If they appear, the reporter has included them.
On Jan. 8, 1930, one Member of Congress referred to the *Congressional Record* as a "catch-all, . . .a burying ground for

editorials, articles, speeches and addresses from all parts of the country relating to every conceivable subject. . ."

Such additions in the body or the Extensions section cost money. According to a staff member of the Joint Committee on Printing, one of the longest *Record* insertions by a Member of the House was made by Rep. Royal C. Johnson (R S.D. 1915-1933), who inserted 504 pages of names of World War I slackers. No figures on the cost of this extension are available.

In 1935, a Senate speech opposing the National Recovery Administration by Sen. Huey Long (D La. 1931-1935) took up 85 pages of the *Record* and cost $4,493. One of the longest insertions was made by Sen. Robert LaFollette (R Wis. 1885-1891, 1905-1925), who on May 5, 1914 inserted a 365-page speech on railroad rates. The cost of printing this extension, according to figures supplied by the Joint Committee on Printing, was $13,760.85.

Attempts to limit what can be added to the *Record* have not been very successful. New York City Mayor John V. Lindsay, then a Member of the House, in 1962 introduced a bill to require that two type faces be used in printing the *Record*—one for the actual debates and the other for all materials subsequently added to the *Record.* The bill, HR 534 was never reported by a committee.

Production Costs, Schedule

Costs.   The cost of producing the *Record* has increased over the years. According to officials at the GPO, the cost per page is determined by dividing the total printed pages of the daily *Record*, the index, the byweekly and bound volumes into the total GPO appropriation for the *Record* in a given fiscal year.

Schedule.   The texts of the Senate and House floor debates, matter for the Extensions and Daily Digest sections are assembled by the GPO each night before printing. The size of the *Record* never can be accurately determined beforehand, since it depends on the length of floor proceedings. The only known fact is that the *Record* must be printed and delivered by 8 a.m., regardless of its size or how late Congress remained in session.

GPO officials said that to their knowledge the *Record* never has missed its morning delivery deadline.

Production begins at 6:30 p.m., when "preparers" check incoming copy, note sections to be printed in specific type sizes and ascertain that the material to be printed is in proper sequential order. The copy is set by nearly 400 composing and casting machines, proofed, corrected and readied for stereotyping by 2 a.m. The double-deck, 64-page rotary magazine presses that print the *Record* are supposed to be in operation by 2:15 a.m., running 18,000 impressions an hour. These presses print 49,000 copies of the *Record* each day, using 36 rolls of paper weighing nearly 21.5 tons.

By 8 a.m., 34,635 copies of the *Record* are delivered to Congressional offices: 100 are hand-delivered to the homes of Members requesting such service in the Washington area; 277 are delivered to area libraries, offices and universities; 6,000 to 7,000 are mailed to individual subscribers; and 5,837 go to federal agencies. Each Senator is allotted 100 copies to distribute free to his constituents; each Representative is allotted 68.

Per-Page Cost of Record
1963-1970

1963	$104.19
1964	96.05
1965	108.50
1966	104.00
1967	110.00
1968	113.00
1969	116.00
1970	119.00
	(est.)

Prior Publications

1789-1790 — The Congressional Register. An early attempt to publish record of Congressional debates. Taken down in shorthand by Thomas Lloyd of New York. Four volumes total.

1790-1825—Debate in House reported in haphazard way by some of better newspapers. Senate debates scarcely reported at all.

1834—Publication of first volume of *Annals of Congress.* Produced by Gales and Seaton. Brought together material from newspapers, magazines and other sources on Congressional proceedings from 1st through 12th Congresses (March 3, 1789, to May 27, 1824). Forty-two volumes total.

1824-1837—Register of Debate. Produced by Gales and Seaton; directly reported Congressional proceedings.

1833-1873 — The Congressional Globe. Published by Blair and Rives. Covered 23rd through 42nd Congresses (Dec. 2, 1833, to March 3, 1873). Forty-six volumes total.

1873 to Present — Congressional Record. Produced by the Government Printing Office.

SCOPE AND BIASES OF NEWSPAPERS AND COLUMNISTS

Ideally newspapers should be objective. That is, they should record what has happened with no hint of bias, no heavy hand of opinion. But such pristine purity is a myth. E. B. White, most sensitive of modern U. S. humor writers, has said that he who puts pen to paper writes, unavoidably, of himself. Reporters and columnists are people, and as such have feelings and convictions that cannot be squeezed to death on the keyboard of the typewriter.

But even if such biases could be dealt with by the individual writer, hundreds of other aspects enter to blur the clean lines of objectivity. The length an editor allows the story to run, for instance, is a form of editorializing. So is the size of the headline placed above the story, and on the particular page itself. The fact that the story was printed and not discarded is the strongest and most obvious form of editorializing, since it calls for a basic opinion from the editor.

To cope with these conscious and subconscious biases, then, one must become aware of the general editorial tone of the publication he is reading.

One newspaper will bend over backwards to play a sensational rape-murder case on page one, while another will discard the story entirely. Others have pet projects or peeves which they continually overplay in their delight or pique; still others show an identifying lack of news judgment and a willingness to be guided in their story selection by the daily wire service log and outside publications.

Another point to be considered is the lack of real competition among newspapers today. Some 11,400 newspapers are published in the United States; about 1,800 are dailies.

Our population has more than doubled between 1910-1960 while the number of dailies dropped by more than one-third due to the economics of change forced by radio and TV. Today many states have not a single city with competing daily newspapers. In fact, daily newspaper competition survives in less than 60 of our cities.

These warnings are given in hope that the undergraduate will become a more critical and discerning reader.

Certain newspapers, like certain wines, are better or of a higher quality than others. This is due to a number of reasons— they emphasize political, economic, and cultural news; they are well written and have technical excellence; they have a tradition of freedom and economic independence; they have a strong editorial page and enterprising staff. In sum, they give careful in-depth coverage of significant events.

Among the top newspapers in the United States, those that have built over the years a reputation for excellent journalism are *The New York Times, Christian Science Monitor, Washington Post, Wall Street Journal,* and the *St. Louis Post Dispatch.*

A large number of small-town newspapers too have extremely good reputations — they are, ironically, pressured in many ways into being a good newspaper precisely because they are in small towns. No reporter or small-city editor can publish anything without being certain that someone will react directly to him, face-to-face. For this reason, when the small-city reporter gets his facts wrong, almost everybody in town knows it; they know the people involved and they probably know of the incident reported.

The big-city reporter does not have this over-the-shoulder check on his work — and, it might be said, is the worse for it.

In May of 1970, a concensus of the American Newspaper Publishers Association decided that in small towns where an editor has no anonymity there's so much rapport between the newspaper and the reader that no one can get away with much. Great metropolitan dailies, on the other hand, can generalize and pervert the news to their own views, and often do, to the utter disregard of truth and fact.

As for their political biases, independently owned newspapers have a right, a duty even, to endorse on editorial pages those running for public office and to crusade for or against any issue that so stirs them. Most daily newspapers, for instance, endorse a presidential candidate or a party ticket during an election campaign.

Table 6 shows how the American dailies shaped up politically during presidential campaigns through the recent years and Table 7 gives the state by state line-up of dailies for the 1968 presidential election.

Table 6

EDITORIAL ENDORSEMENT OF PRESIDENTIAL CANDIDATES BY UNITED STATES DAILY NEWSPAPERS

	% Papers		% Circulation
		1944	
Dewey	60		68.5
Roosevelt	22		17.7
Uncommitted	18		13.8
		1948	
Dewey	65		78.5
Truman	15		10
Others	4		1.5
Uncommitted	16		10
		1952	
Eisenhower	67		80
Stevenson	14.5		11
Uncommitted	18.5		9
		1956	
Eisenhower	63		72
Stevenson	15		13
Uncommitted	23		15
		1960	
Nixon	57.7		70.9
Kennedy	16.4		15.8
Uncommitted	25.9		13.3
		1964	
Goldwater	34.7		20.5
Johnson	42.4		62
Uncommitted	22.9		17.5
		1968	
Nixon	60.8		69.9
Humphrey	14		19.3
Wallace	1.2		.3
Uncommitted	24		10.5

Source: *Editor & Publisher*, Newspaper Trade Journal. November 5, 1960; October 31, 1964; November 2, 1968.

Table 7

STATE-BY-STATE LINEUP OF DAILIES

State	Nixon No.	Nixon Circ.	Humphrey No.	Humphrey Circ.	Wallace No.	Wallace Circ.	Independent or Uncommitted No.	Independent or Uncommitted Circ.
Alabama	4	289,327	1	19,270	5	74,601	2	27,747
Alaska	3	42,920	1	12,605	:	.....	1	1,931
Arizona	3	206,626	1	39,791	:	.....	3	106,905
Arkansas	5	128,273	3	117,438	1	4,526	3	13,486
California	60	4,093,468	12	670,451	:	.....	12	215,270
Colorado	8	271,182	4	281,281	1	1,215	3	77,254
Connecticut	6	498,626	:	.....	:	.....	7	200,443
Delaware	2	132,405	:	.....	:	.....	1	18,656
Dist. Columbia	2	535,119	:	.....	:	.....	:	.....
Florida	31	1,499,261	5	182,770	:	.....	1	19,432
Georgia	13	299,995	5	525,936	:	.....	4	32,370
Hawaii	1	112,182	1	67,550	:	.....	:	.....
Idaho	8	105,868	2	24,361	:	.....	2	21,467
Illinois	38	3,400,816	3	46,549	:	.....	13	151,912
Indiana	29	637,975	10	122,772	:	.....	12	353,776
Iowa	17	207,039	3	379,967	:	.....	6	93,323
Kansas	30	547,584	1	5,677	:	.....	3	17,476
Kentucky	7	90,004	6	455,793	:	.....	5	47,600

Table 7 (continued)

State	Nixon No.	Nixon Circ.	Humphrey No.	Humphrey Circ.	Wallace No.	Wallace Circ.	Independent or Uncommitted No.	Independent or Uncommitted Circ.
Louisiana	6	243,256	::	......	1	11,303	7	240,986
Maine	2	112,465	::	......	:	......	3	92,780
Maryland	8	706,460	::	......	:	......	1	21,461
Massachusetts	12	452,153	4	562,337	:	......	10	345,257
Michigan	19	1,818,514	::	......	:	......	6	172,737
Minnesota	8	92,406	6	782,195	:	......	4	111,581
Mississippi	3	41,314	1	13,523	3	60,749	3	49,209
Missouri	14	910,979	4	376,899	1	7,130	13	412,979
Montana	7	115,882	2	47,713	:	......	1	2,132
Nebraska	12	416,529	2	37,161	:	......	2	8,362
Nevada	1	22,825	1	19,323	:	......	::	......
New Hampshire	4	76,714	1	9,249	:	......	2	19,971
New Jersey	17	1,038,964	6	509,992	:	......	1	59,243
New Mexico	6	117,848	2	22,372	:	......	4	19,346
New York	40	4,125,442	11	2,110,121	:	......	10	655,037
North Carolina	10	391,284	3	180,021	:	......	17	341,924
North Dakota	7	125,742	::	......	:	......	::	......
Ohio	35	2,532,965	2	168,110	:	......	12	136,154
Oklahoma	4	482,257	4	15,131	:	......	10	61,002
Oregon	10	495,329	1	14,918	:	......	3	25,561

Pennsylvania	39	1,875,593	4	387,539	:	:	21	406,356
Rhode Island	3	233,780	:	.....	:	:	:	.....
South Carolina	5	332,253	1	52,670	:	:	4	66,738
South Dakota	4	107,111	1	13,600	:	:	1	3,460
Tennessee	12	733,204	4	227,773	:	:	4	54,265
Texas	22	1,725,518	12	445,548	:	:	17	171,627
Utah	1	108,566	:	.....	:	:	3	109,558
Vermont	4	54,754	1	7,596	:	:	1	6,031
Virginia	15	577,948	2	26,441	:	:	7	157,602
Washington	12	759,234	:	.....	:	:	:	.....
West Virginia	7	129,789	6	120,426	:	:	1	8,536
Wisconsin	15	486,609	4	445,138	:	:	2	32,787
Wyoming	3	27,046	3	24,941	:	:	2	10,025
Total Responding Newspapers and Their Circulation	634	34,559,385	146	9,572,948	12	159,524	250	5,201,845
Percent of Total	60.8%	69.9%	14.0%	19.3%	1.2%	.3%	24.0%	10.5%

Twenty Major Political Columnists

In twenty years the events of the present will have been digested, analyzed, interpreted, and reinterpreted by a host of writers and academicans. But one need not wait until news is history to place it in an intelligent perspective. This is the job of the political columnist, who brings his extensive background and experience to the task of making sense out of today's news. Every American newspaper features several of these columnists, but their work varies in two important ways: by their political and ideological bias, and by the columnist's standard of relevance, that is, the news on which he chooses to focus.

Many columnists can be identified with one of the major political parties, and most can be placed somewhere on the American ideological spectrum. This bias is important because columnists specialize in instant analysis, which often cannot be double-checked. It is especially helpful to identify those columnists who have developed a reputation for independence and objectivity. Each columnist, regardless of his political bias, has his own sense of what is relevant, his own focus on the news. For instance, Walter Lippmann is philosophical, Jack Anderson looks for the behind-the-scenes exposé, and Jimmy Breslin stresses the human element in politics. The spectrum of American political columnists offers literally something for everyone, but one must know where to look. The following description of twenty major columnists includes liberals, conservatives, and independents, and identifies the particular scope and focus of each.

Joseph Alsop

Joseph Alsop's column appears three days a week in newspapers across the nation, and until quite recently it has always carried a message of doom concerning the country's foreign policy. Alsop spends his column inches predicting the imminent collapse of the American political system, and if he is wrong, it is not because he did not do his homework. During his more than thirty years on Capitol Hill he has gained a reputation for hard work, single-minded thoroughness, and dogmatism.

Alsop dropped his doomsday theme when the war in Vietnam took a serious turn, and he has been one of the few top newsmen in the world predicting an American military victory there. Watching

Alsop in action in Vietnam, Everett Martin of *Newsweek* remarked, "He didn't get briefed by colonels, he briefed them."

Another of Alsop's specialties is that of predicting the future. Long before 1968 he predicted the birth of the 1968 Wallace third-party movement and the revival of the Southern Democrat-Conservative Republican coalition. The earmark of a typical Alsop column is a studied depth of background fused into a message of gloom.

Right or wrong, Joseph Alsop is seldom ignored in Washington. Over the years his predictions have been accurate often enough to demand serious consideration.

Jack Anderson

Drew Pearson and Jack Anderson wrote the daily column "The Washington Merry-Go-Round," printed in over 600 newspapers around the country, for more than twenty-five years. Anderson has continued the column alone since Pearson's death. As a column, it stands alone.

Pearson and Anderson have exposed more wrongdoing leading to actual court convictions or formal censure than all other Washington columnists combined.

It was this pair of writers who brought the focus of public opinion and, later, that of the courts on General Harry Vaughn in the Truman administration, on Sherman Adams and Bernard Goldfine in the Eisenhower administration, and on Bobby Baker, Adam Clayton Powell, and Thomas Dodd in the Johnson administration.

Although Pearson and Anderson have attacked corruption in both parties and in individuals of all ideologies, their causes tend to be liberal ones: removal of the oil depletion allowance, regulation of highway billboards, promotion of the United Nations, and support of civil rights. The two characteristics of a Pearson-Anderson column are "inside" verbatim dialogue, the actual occurrence of which is difficult to prove, and the use of the column to pressure individuals systematically. Their attacks are daily ones—sometimes strong, sometimes trivial—but unrelenting.

Because Anderson has no large paid staff, he uses the column to lure inside information, much of it being technically unsolicited. In this way the column's notoriety has worked well for him. Many reporters who want to see a particular news story in print—a story that their own newspapers would not risk printing—often turn it over to Anderson.

Russell Baker

Armed with an unfailing sense of humor, *New York Times* syndicated columnist Russell Baker roams the countryside in search of windmills. When he finds one worthy of his lance, he quickly selects its weakest point and lunges ahead.

His writings are heavily laced with satire and he observes no sacred cows. As unbelievable as some of his columns are, they usually come close to some embarrasing truth. In a column on the black militants H. Rap Brown and Stokeley Carmichael, he leaked the "inside" news that Brown "is an undercover agitator on the payroll of the Senate Appropriations Committee." He said Brown's job was to find cheap solutions to the nation's racial problems. Carmichael supposedly was a Senate aide who got tired of tedious office chores and was assigned to save Congress money by reducing support for the Civil Rights movement. Baker quotes his imaginary Congressional source: "The fact is that some problems are so difficult we can't do much about them ... still the public expects us to come up with the answers. As long as we have a few Rap Browns working for us we can be certain of having an answer when the public wants it."

Baker's wanderings between fact and fiction leave a provocative trail. Usually his fiction is more real than the news on page one.

Jimmy Breslin

Formerly a columnist for the *New York Post*, Jimmy Breslin is also the author of a novel, *The Gang That Couldn't Shoot Straight.* Currently, he writes for the weekly magazine *New York.* His particular emphasis is the emotional impact of issues rather than the issues themselves.

Although in the past Breslin's column dealt with Runyonesque characters (like Marvin the Torch and Fat Thomas), he now applies his personal approach to national issues. Breslin even took a plunge into politics as Norman Mailer's running mate in the 1969 New York mayoralty primary.

He recently visited Vietnam with *New York Times* pundit James Reston. In striking contrast to Reston's interviews with diplomats and generals, Breslin talked with ordinary GI's: "Lodge and Dean Rusk and those people are not my set ..." he explained. "I regard the whole scene like the 16th precinct in Manhattan. I don't get involved with anybody but the arresting officer and the desk sergeant."

In 1967 Congress lightly dismissed a rat-control bill. While the main body of the big-name columnists solemnly deplored the inadequacies of Congress, Breslin spent the night in a rat-infested tenement. His vivid column was reprinted in the *Congressional Record*, and it set the tone for the later reconsideration and passage of the bill.

Breslin has been called a throwback—a man reporting in a style that went out with the speakeasy. But, no matter how sophisticated journalism has become, there is still a need for this kind of human-impact reporting.

David Broder

Broder attempts to fill the gap between the academic political scientist writing about the political systems and the reporter-columnist writing about personalities and events. He does this by covering areas that are usually ignored by both textbooks and newspapers: national party apparatus, local party leaders, campaign organizations, and the complexities of the national convention.

It was he who emphasized Nixon's strategy of "deliberate delay" in locking up the Republican nomination, and his supporters' "unusual tactic of seeking not commitments for their man, but pledges that the delegates would be unpledged to anyone."

Occasionally Broder scores an important news beat. When TV reporters asked Richard Nixon if anyone had forecast his selection of Spiro T. Agnew as a running mate, Nixon said, "Well, yes, Dave Broder did."

The most important feature of Broder's column is analysis. As do most political scientists, he sees politics as a system. Unlike most academicians, however, Broder has a weekly column in which to air his ideas, and he speaks with clarity to the general public. "If I have any strong conviction about national politics," Broder has said, "it is that it's essentially local politics. The pros at Miami Beach thought first and foremost of the effect back home of decisions made at the convention."

Art Buchwald

Nothing is sacred to Art Buchwald, whose column, "Capitol Punishment," is the most widely syndicated humor column in the world (printed even in *Pravda* and *Isvestia*). His technique is to take a complex situation and, by playing the role of a very naive analyst, reduce the issue to its logical absurdity. An example is his explanation of Lyndon Johnson's selection of Hubert Humphrey as Vice-President: "One day, while he [LBJ] was eating lunch with Mrs. Johnson, she said to him, 'You know, Lyndon, we owe the Humphreys a dinner.' And the President said, 'Ah don't have time to have dinner with the Humphreys, but ah tell you what, Lady Bird, ah'll make it up to them some way!'"

Buchwald provides more than comic relief; his columns are sharply pointed and deeply revealing, as well as humorous. His satiric attacks on the people and events that make up the news serve to point out the political absurdities of the present that should make one angry.

William Buckley

Buckley has brought style, verve, humor, and intellect to conservative political commentary. His column is unique. His conservative views are usually predictable: opposition to most government welfare programs, to the graduated income tax, to federal support of racial integration, and to the UN; and support for strong prosecution of the war in Vietnam and the most conservative candidate around (although not George Wallace).

Buckley habitually and vigorously defends the latest public scapegoat whom other columnists consider indefensible: for example, Joseph McCarthy, Roy Cohen, Barry Goldwater, Ronald Reagan, Lyndon Johnson, Thomas Dodd, or Spiro Agnew. Some of his views are not reconcilable with conventional conservatism, for Buckley is a philosophical conservative (and at times a libertarian) with no pretense of practicality. He opposes snooping census takers, will consider the negative income tax, has some sympathy for ghetto control of local schools, and denounces Robert Welch of the John Birch Society.

Buckley is at his best when fighting liberals with their own weapons—quotations from Thomas Jefferson, analogy, classical allusions, and devastating wit.When John Kenneth Galbraith appeared on a picket line of striking telephone employees to demonstrate his support, Buckley commented: "It was a nostalgic demonstration of an old faith, rather as if Marlene Dietrich emulating the Victorian ladies of yesteryear were to faint upon hearing an obscenity."

Buckley seldom spends time developing his ideas fully; therefore, he seldom brings any fresh information to his reader. He is rather an idea broker who handles his ideas roughly or gently depending on his whim, and this he does very well.

Marquis Childs

Marquis Childs writes full-length essays that appear as newspaper columns, and they are distinguished by their completeness. Unlike the newer style of columns, which emphasize only opinions, Childs does not take his readers' backgrounds for granted. When he evaluated Hubert Humphrey's chances in Michigan in 1968, for example, his column was typically 35 percent longer than most, and it was also a short course in Michigan politics.

This thorough approach is understandable, for Childs is also an established author with several best sellers to his credit. In the early 1930's he attended a housing conference in Scandinavia and became so interested in the Swedish experiment in non-Marxist socialism that he wrote the best seller *Sweden: The Middle Way* (New Haven, Conn.: Yale University Press, 1936). Since then, he has written a number of other books, including *Eisenhower: Captive Hero* (New York: Harcourt Brace, 1958), and several political novels, the latest being *Taint of Conscience* (New York: Harper & Row, Publishers, 1967), about international spying.

Childs' liberal orientation goes back to Franklin Roosevelt and the New Deal. Despite his long identification with liberal causes, he is not an insider to the "liberal establishment." Childs' idealism has kept him from the inner circle, for John F. Kennedy was friendly to tough-minded Joseph Alsop and Lyndon Johnson confided in elite-oriented William S. White. Childs has supported liberal Democratic goals since the early 1930s, but he has never accepted the bargaining and the deals that politicians feel are necessary to accomplish them. His columns and his books have an idealistic and independent tinge. Frequently he tends to write somewhat "off the news," discussing a threat to privacy or civil liberties while a world crisis is dominating the headlines.

Roscoe Drummond

Roscoe Drummond launched his political column in the mid-1920's; early in 1969 his son Geoffrey's name was added to the by-line— only to be deleted one year later when the young Drummond died. The father, older now but as sure-footed as ever, once again shoulders full responsibility for the column.

The chief characteristic of a Drummond column is that it is not easy to categorize. Believing that government policies should be "expounded faithfully before they are attacked earnestly," the column does not fit into any ideological niche. Its two distinguishing features are a policy orientation, rather than a personality or ideological one, and a balanced objective style. The Drummond belief that policies deserve a fair hearing before they are criticized makes it often the best source for a clear systematic explanation of a new policy. Roscoe Drummond's criterion of a "fair hearing" has led Republicans to call him a Democrat and Democrats to charge that he is a Republican. Drummond states that Pierre Salinger was amazed at the fair coverage he gave John F. Kennedy at the start of his quest for the presidential nomination, because many Democrats were sure that Drummond was a Republican in view of the fact that he had written so many columns explaining Eisenhower's policy.

As a reporter, editor, and Washington bureau chief for the *Christian Science Monitor*, Drummond absorbed a good deal of that journal's "passion for objectivity." It is a passion that has paid off in the trust shown him by many government officials who, wanting a fair, concise exposition of a new policy, release it to Drummond first. Examples are President Nixon's revelation of his concept of an agency for human resources and President Eisenhower's endorsement of Nixon in 1968 before the Republican convention.

The Drummond focus on policy, rather than on personalities or ideology, makes him an unusual columnist in another way, in that most policy-oriented columnists have a liberal Democratic point of view, and most conservative columnists are both more conservative than the Nixon administration and primarily interested in personalities and ideology. This configuration, then, gives Drummond an almost clear field for policy exposition during the Nixon presidency.

Rowland Evans and Robert Novack

Evans and Novack's "Inside Report" is the fastest rising political column in the United States. In an interview with Julius Duscha in *Potomac* magazine, both men characterized their column as a "reporting" rather than an interpreting column, as Novack explained:

> I think editors are surfeited with armchair opinion and are crying for reasonably accurate, factual reporting on politics. What we are really trying to do is intersect the lines of communication in Washington. Anyone who has enough energy can do it . . . We just sort of scramble. It makes people feel they know what

is going on inside. We take a strong point of view on a situation, but we're not strongly doctrinaire. Neither Rowly nor I is terribly profound. I don't think we're in business to point up the good; we're trying to show the foibles of people. The conservatives claim that we're a liberal column and the liberals claim that we're a conservative column, which I think shows that we're doing a good job of stepping on a lot of toes.

Evans further commented, "We think there's a conflict everywhere, and our job is to find it and reveal it. And I know damned well there's conflict in heaven." In the five years since their column originated, Evans and Novack have exposed a good deal of conflict.

Many of their columns are devoted to the machinery of organized politics. They were the first to describe Richard Nixon's well developed national organization for capturing the Republican nomination. Later, they broke the first big story of the Nixon administration by revealing several days before the formal announcement that Melvin Laird was to be Secretary of Defense.

Time magazine has characterized them as the "Zealots of the Middle," because they attack extremists of both the right and the left. Their discovery of a John Birch Society member in the "President's Club," an exclusive organization for large Democratic campaign contributors, led to a resignation and a refund of a $12,000 donation. On the other hand they have attacked black power militants in SNCC and defended former OEO boss Sargent Shriver in a battle with black militants over control of the poverty program in Mississippi.

Art Hoppe

This San Francisco humor columnist, not always happy with the world as it is reported in the rest of the newspaper, has succeeded in creating one of his own. Hoppe's world is really no better than the real world, but in it selfishness, stupidity, and hypocrisy are easier to identify.

Hope uses all the common weapons in a humorist's arsenal, exaggeration, pathos, and logical absurdity, to explode the pomposity of the world as he sees it. He employs these weapons in a continuing series of fables, parables, and mythical organizations. One of his columns begins:

One of the most burning moral issues of our time is capital punishment. And after carefully weighing the arguments on both sides, I'd like to say a few words about the death penalty: It isn't enough. The purpose of the death penalty, everybody agrees, is to show killers that killing people is bad. Which we do by killing them. And that sure shows them. But is this example effective on potential killers? Not very. Because no matter how many people we kill to show people that killing people is bad, people still go on killing people. Obviously then, the death penalty alone isn't a strong enough deterrent. And after much thought, I have formed the Bring Back the Rack Committee, a do-good organization.

Hoppe's bias is generally liberal, and like many social critics, he can be quite self-righteous. His nationally syndicated column, however, is quite enjoyable, and it brings to light the ultimate absurdity of many American policies.

James Kilpatrick

For many years James Kilpatrick was for the Old South the most literate and articulate defender of racial segregation. His editorials in the *Richmond News Leader* led to national prominence and, eventually, to a television debate with Martin Luther King, Jr.

Kilpatrick defended segregation from the position of an elite conservative—one who valued the genteel life of "the good old days" as he remembered them and who did not want to see them changed. His gentility did not prevent him from making frankly racist appeals. For example, he once wrote, "The Negro is fundamentally and perhaps unalterably inferior; he is immoral, indolent, inept, incapable of learning, and uninterested in full racial equality. The segregationist South feels no guilt about keeping the Negro in his place...."

Today Kilpatrick's column has changed, and segregation is no longer a topic. Still, his innate conservatism serves as a useful basis for a general political column. Kilpatrick has a crisp, elegant style, and when he finds stupidity and mismanagement in the world around him, he attacks it with real force. Like William Buckley, he also defends those under attack by the liberal establishment.

Joseph Kraft

Kraft, who was a Phi Beta Kappa at Columbia University and spent a year at Princeton's Institute for Advanced Study, writes a thoughtful philosophical column stressing the complexity of political problems and the necessity for more than common sense and clear thinking to solve them. He is the journalistic link to the new breed of "policy intellectuals" who are playing a growing role in governmental decision-making.

His column on the Supreme Court criminal confession decisions ignored the usual arguments and stressed, instead, how little is really known about the operation of the criminal justice system and the usually accepted link between confessions and convictions—a conclusion later confirmed by the President's Crime Commission Report.

Kraft generally supports liberal goals (he was a speech writer for John F. Kennedy) but refuses to be classified as a liberal. In fact, while supporting the goals of Kennedy and Johnson, he was also quite critical of their "shortsightedness" in meeting those goals. Kraft is one of the first men to bring to a newspaper column the resources of policy-oriented intellectuals—an approach that will become more and more important in a "post-industrial" society in which the university is the dominant institution.

David Lawrence

Having written a syndicated Washington column since 1916, David Lawrence is the acknowledged dean of Washington correspondents. He is also the unquestioned voice of conventional conservatism. It is important to realize that Lawrence is the publisher of the U. S. *News & World Report,* and is, therefore, likely to maintain the conservative line in all areas of policy. His columns generally fall neatly into two categories: exposition and opinion. On the strength of his half-century in Washington, Lawrence is able to make such subtle political comparisons as that of James Cox's fate as heir to a failing Wilson administration in 1920 with Hubert Humphrey's plight in 1968. His longevity has given him an instinct for the voter's feelings that is not always matched by professional pollsters.

Generally, Lawrence is as predictable as the planets. His policy position is very near that of the more conservative Republicans and Southern Democrats. That is to say, he supports the war in Vietnam, opposes foreign aid and other foreign entanglements, suspects most domestic spending programs, and deplores the most recent Supreme Court decisions. His is a reliable, conservative opinion.

Walter Lippmann

For many years Walter Lippmann's column, "Today and Tommorrow," provided a perspective of history in the form of journalism of today. It is difficult to describe the full impact of Lippmann upon American political leaders. James Reston, himself a respected reporter and columnist, pointed out that when Lippmann returned from a trip to Russia and Germany "his reports were part of the common conversation of the Capitol. Every embassy up and down Sixteenth Street and Massachusetts Avenue discussed them and reported them to their governments. Members of the Senate Foreign Relations Committee read them and questioned the Secretary of State on his points."

Walter Lippmann seems to be able to interpret the intentions of American policy better than can the official policy-makers themselves. Patrick O'Donovan of the *London Observer* writes, "State Department officials answering general questions in private quite often say 'Have you read Lippmann on that?'"

Lippmann has earned this praise and influence in a journalistic career that began under the tutelage of Lincoln Steffens in 1912. In the decades that followed, Lippmann wrote a number of books, many of which are required reading in college courses today: *Public Opinion* (New York: Crowell-Collier-Macmillan, 1922); *Preface to Politics* (New York: Crowell-Collier-Macmillan, 1933); *Essays in the Public Philosophy* (Boston: Little, Brown, 1955); *Draft and Mastery* (Englewood Cliffs, N. J.: Prentice-Hall, 1961), to name but a few.

Lippmann has had such influence because he is an original political thinker. In his own words, he has "lived two lives," one of philosophy that provides the context of his day-to-day observation on men and events, and one of journalism that provides the "laboratory" in which to test the philosophy and keep it from becoming too abstract. As a political thinker he has grappled with such fundamental political issues as elite leadership in a democracy, the formulation of issues, the relevance of liberal democracy in the twentieth century, natural law, the limitations of public opinion, and isolationism.

It is impossible to place Lippman on the usual political spectrum because he has endorsed Republicans and Democrats and has been conservative on one issue and liberal on another. Yet, he remains so singularly judicious that he neither offends nor enrages his opponents. In his careful weighing and balancing of factors that shape great issues he is rarely entirely satisfactory to partisans of either side. On the most important issue of the late 1960's, the Vietnam war, he was an early opponent of American policy and reluctantly endorsed Richard Nixon as the best hope of withdrawal.

For over forty years Lippmann's columns, first in the *New York World* and later the *New York Herald Tribune*, have provided the intellectual agenda for those who wish to understand public policy. Today his column appears only fortnightly in *Newsweek*, but, in James Reston's words, he is still able to "put the events of the day in its proper relationship to the history of yesterday and the dream of tomorrow."

Mary McGrory

Mary McGrory writes about the human factor behind behavior. "I have very few opinions," she has said, "but powerful impressions." It is these impressions that she offers in her column, "Point of View." Her style has been called the "poet's gift of analogy," an effect she creates by combining classical literary allusions with current feeling and events.

She gained national recognition for her descriptions of the Army-McCarthy hearings in the early 1950's. She commented that Senator Joseph McCarthy's counsel, Roy Cohen, "looked like a boy who has had a letter sent home from school about him and has come back to his elders to get the whole thing straightened out."

Rather than the direct and recognizable influence of Lippmann or Reston, Miss McGrory has a subtle and indirect influence on attitudes. Her writing reflects the feelings that most people have but cannot express as well. Her description of the then Vice-President Richard Nixon has become a standard one among other reporters and commentators: "He still stalks the light touch with all the grimness that butterfly collectors bring to the pursuit of a rare specimen." Miss McGrory now writes for the *Washington Star* and is nationally syndicated.

James Reston

James "Scotty" Reston is perhaps America's most outstanding columnist. A reporter in the Washington Bureau of the *New York Times*, he writes a column of stunning significance and perception. His columns deal with likely and specific consequences of political actions. He discusses why a particular event happened and what else will happen as a result. For this reason his political bias is difficult to identify.

Reston believes in the primacy of journalism and in this light frequently asks embarrassing questions of even his friends in political circles. Among the Washington Press Corps he is the acknowledged master of the bluff, of extracting facts from officials by pretending he already knows the whole story (and often enough, with the aid of the *Times* bureau, he does).

Reston uses his resources skillfully, not only to report and interpret the news, but also to influence it. William Rivers, in *The Opinion-Makers*, notes instances in presidential administrations going back to Franklin Roosevelt in which Reston directly or indirectly influenced political events. Reston is a political realist. He respects politicans who can operate effectively while living up to their own ideals, and he criticizes those who fall short of this standard. His wit is scathing, his criticism unerring, and his judgement impartial. He described Nelson Rockefeller in 1963: "Nelson Rockefeller was in Washington but his old friends hardly recognized him. He talked like Harold Stassen and acted like Richard Nixon. The presidential bug has really got him. You could tell because he really denied it." He also flailed John F. Kennedy by declaring: "He has talked like Churchill, acted like Chamberlin." Of Humber Humphrey after his 1968 defeat Reston remarked: "The trouble with Hubert Humphrey is that he won't quit while he is behind or enjoy the pleasures of defeat."

The reader of a Reston column may be sure of two things: official Washington will be talking about it that day, and within a week other columnists will be writing on the same subject.

Cyrus Leo Sulzberger

New York Times columnist Cy Sulzberger has been covering international events for almost thirty years. His experiences as chief of the *New York Times* foreign correspondents has given him a well-defined philosophy of the world, which he has never been hesitant to phrase: "Our business is neither ideological warfare nor the rigid maintenance of any status quo. Our business is to protect our own national interests from any threat, regardless of its philosophical label, and to try and see that changes in an ever-changing world are sufficiently controlled to avoid excessively dangerous explosions."

With the exception of his many columns on Vietnam, Sulzberger usually writes somewhat "off the news." He tries to bring particular events into a general framework and to prepare his readers for future flareups. Writing about the Czech crisis, for instance, he said that the real crisis was for the Russians. "Unless they can apply some of the changes pioneered in Czechoslovakia, the whole system will collapse."

Sulzberger and Joseph Alsop are the two major columnists defending the Vietnam war who cannot be identified as conservatives. Sulzberger puts Vietnam in world perspective—his own world perspective, to be sure—but it is still an overall view. The United

States, he feels, has a continuing responsibility to live up to the role of world super-power, which it inherited in 1945: "The 1947 Greek commitment under the Truman Doctrine was also originally unpopular. Many naïve Americans and their newspapers then preferred the Communist rebels to the Athens government. . . . If we crawl out of Vietnam now, it is obvious that Southeast Asia right down to Australia will join our adversaries and that India will be outflanked." It is important to note that Sulzberger's "power politics internationalist" viewpoint has been held in both the Pentagon and the State Department.

William S. White

White admires men of power, but not dissenters, such as Senator Eugene McCarthy or Robert Kennedy. He writes about elite politics, focusing on the problem of inner-circle negotiations. His interest in political professionals has naturally made him a great admirer of Lyndon Johnson and, in fact, the title of his laudatory Johnson biography is *The Professional* (Boston: Houghton Mifflin, 1964).

His sympathy and understanding for the problems of powerful leaders has paid off with access and friendships that cross party lines to have included Robert Taft, Dwight Eisenhower, Lyndon Johnson, and Richard Nixon.

White has an ability to discover and write about those obscure facets of personality that allow one leader to develop a rapport with another. When he leaves the inner circle of elite politics, however, his power of analysis weakens and blinds him to the popular appeal of such men as Robert Kennedy, William Fulbright, or Eugene McCarthy. He should be read for his exclusive access to and deep understanding of leaders—particularly with regard to Nixon—but his strong bias must be kept in mind.

Tom Wicker

Tom Wicker's special contribution as a columnist is his ability to identify problem situations before they emerge. He inherited the venerable Arthur Krock's "In the Nation" column on the editorial page of the *New York Times* and has given the column his own special emphasis.

Wicker travels widely, attempting to identify local situations that will have a national significance. In 1966 he attended a political rally in Pioneer Park, Wyoming, and described the crowd's reaction to national, state, and local candidates. In doing so he identified and brought to life many political science generalizations about campaigning that usually remain buried in textbooks. That same year he wrote a three-column series on the "guaranteed annual income," which was a thoroughly sophisticated but understandable exposition of a very complex issue. Wicker's columns are more readable and exhibit greater force than the usual objective exposition, because he is not reluctant to take sides. He selected the annual income topic because he was favorably inclined toward the idea. In explaining his position he related the proposal to ideas and values that already were familiar to his readers: "Guaranteed annual income is not something for nothing at all, but an idea that basically confirms the American reluctance to put people on the dole and the American belief in helping people to help themselves."

As part of the *Times* Washington bureau, he covers many of the usual newsmaking events, such as presidential press conferences, but generally he leaves the straight news stories to others and concentrates on analyzing the forces behind the events.

Wicker definitely favors liberal causes, such as massive urban programs and civil rights. He was also an early and vociferous critic of the Vietnam war. His column on the Chicago police during the 1968 Democratic convention was one of the first to attack police behavior, and it still stands as one of the strongest indictments of that situation.